INSTRUMENT MECHANIC FIRST YEAR MCQ

OBJECTIVE QUESTION ANSWERS

MANOJ DOLE

Copyright © Manoj Dole
All Rights Reserved.

This book has been published with all efforts taken to make the material error-free after the consent of the author. However, the author and the publisher do not assume and hereby disclaim any liability to any party for any loss, damage, or disruption caused by errors or omissions, whether such errors or omissions result from negligence, accident, or any other cause.

While every effort has been made to avoid any mistake or omission, this publication is being sold on the condition and understanding that neither the author nor the publishers or printers would be liable in any manner to any person by reason of any mistake or omission in this publication or for any action taken or omitted to be taken or advice rendered or accepted on the basis of this work. For any defect in printing or binding the publishers will be liable only to replace the defective copy by another copy of this work then available.

Digitization is the need of the time. In the future, training in industrial training institutes will need to be conducted using online internet to make training more convenient and easy. E-books containing a set of MCQ questions will be made available to the trainees as they need to be more accustomed to the multiple choice questions MCQ to prepare for the online exams taking place in their industrial training institutes.

With all these factors in mind, Mr. Manoj Madhukar Dole Instructor, Industrial Training Institute, Satara, has written books according to the new annual system and NSQF-5 syllabus. And they've created theoretical mobile apps and blogs to make training easier, and made all these educational materials available for download on the world famous websites Google Play Store, Amazon and Apple Book Store.

The books were published by Hon'ble Joint Director Shri Rajendra Ghume Saheb Regional Office of Vocational Education and Training, Pune on 9/1/2019, at this time Shri Prakash Saigavkar Saheb Principal Government Industrial Training Institute Aundh Pune, Shri Tukaram Misal Saheb Principal Govt. Q. Sanstha Satara, Shri Sachin Dhumal Saheb District Vocational Education and Training Officer Satara, Shri Yatin Pargaonkar Saheb Principal Govt. Q. Sanstha Kolhapur, Shri Vikas Teke Saheb Inspector Vocational Education and Training Regional Office Pune, Palekar Foods Products Pvt. Ltd. Entrepreneurial Chairman of Satara Mr. Nilkanthrao Palekar Saheb, Chairman of Hira Foods Mr. Ibrahim Baba Tamboli Saheb, Mrs. Shalmali Pawar Headmaster Government Technical School Center Satara and other dignitaries were present on the occasion.

Contents

Prologue

Instrument Mechanic First Year MCQ is a simple Book for ITI & Engineering Course Instrument Mechanic First Year, Revised NSQF Syllabus, It contains objective questions with underlined & bold correct answers MCQ covering all topics including all about the latest & Important about safety and environment, use of fire extinguishers, artificial respiratory resuscitation to begin with. He gets the idea of trade tools & its standardization, Familiarize with basics of electricity, construction of PMMC & MI instruments. Overhauling and testing & calibration of ammeters, voltmeters, wattmeter and ampere-hour meter of various types, meter sensitivity, accuracy, maximum power, capability

etc. Test the cable and measure the electrical parameter, experiments on transformer, measuring current and voltage in primary and secondary windings filing practice, marking & measuring with the help of Vernier Caliper, Vernier Height Gauge. Skilling practice on different types & combination of cells for operation and maintenance of batteries being done. Identify and test passive and active electronic components. Construct and test unregulated and regulated power supplies. Practice soldering and de-soldering of various types of electrical and electronic components on through hole PCBs and different type of switches, application like buzzers, solenoid valves. construct and test different types of diode, V-I characteristics, rectifiers, amplifier, op-amps, oscillator and wave shaping circuits. Testing of power electronic components. Construct and test power control circuits. Identify and test opto electronic devices. Able to achieve the skill on SMD Soldering and De-soldering of discrete SMD components. Verifying the truth tables of various digital ICs by referring Data book. Verification of truth tables of various logic gates, RS and JK flip flops, Counters, BCD to decimal decoder, 7 segment display circuits, D/A and A/D circuit, RS485 to RS232 converter. Practice circuit simulation software to simulate and test various circuits. Assemble a computer system, install OS, Practice with MS office. Use the internet, browse, create mail IDs, download desired data from internet using search engines. Familiarization with microprocessor trainer kit, basic program on microprocessor. Measurement voltage, frequency using CRO, operating storage oscilloscope. and lots more.

We add new question answers with each new version. Please email us in case of any errors/omissions. This is arguably the largest and best e-Book for All engineering multiple choice questions and answers.

As a student you can use it for your exam prep. This e-Book is also useful for professors to refresh material.

Foreword

Vocational education and training is imparted through the Department of Vocational Education and Training through the Department of Business Education and Business Practical to supply multi-skilled artisans in line with the rapidly growing demand in the industrial sector in the 21st century. All the occupations within the institutions are important, as the trainees from these occupations develop multi-skills as per the demands of the industry.

with the noble intention of making available MCQ e-books suitable for all businesses, considering that all the examinations in all the industries in the industrial sector are conducted online and include MCQ method questions. Mr. Manoj Madhukar Dole has written a very good e-book on MCQ method as per the new annual syllabus. This e-book will definitely be a guide for all the trainees, trainee candidates, training instructors and others concerned.

The author of the book is Mr. Manoj Madhukar Dole, Instructor Gov. ITI Satara has 17 years of training experience. Written as a new annual pattern, this e-book incorporates modern digital QR Code technology to understand the layout, simple language, and simple syntax, diagrams and videos for each subject. So I am sure that this e-book will definitely be useful for in-depth study and exam practice. The work they have done is certainly commendable.

Mr. Tukaram Misal
Principal Government Industrial Training Institute Satara.

Preface

DGET New Delhi and CSTARI Kolkata have been implementing an annual pattern for all businesses in ITI since the August 2018 session. The examination system will also be changed and it will be online from this year and since all the questions are of Objective Type (MCQ), the trainees are in dire need of in-depth study. It is with this in mind that we are delighted to present the books based on the old NIMI pattern and a complete overview of the new annual pattern, and we hope that these books will be a guide for all business directors and trainees. Is.

For writing these books, Johar Awate Saheb, Principal of ITI Akluj. Former Principal of ITI Satara Saigavkar Saheb, Assistant Director Shri Chandrakant Dhekne Saheb Regional Office of Vocational Education and Training, Pune, District Vocational Education and Training Officer Sachin Dhumal Saheb and Headmaster Government Technical School Kendra Shalmali Pawar Madam and son Adhiraj Dole, mother Kusum Dole, I am very grateful to my father Madhukar Dole and wife Ashwini Dole for their special guidance and cooperation from time to time.

Also, in a very short period of time, the book was reviewed by Shri Rajendra Ghume Saheb, Joint Director, Vocational Education and Training Regional Office, Pune, for his invaluable time in publishing the book. I am sincerely grateful for their feedback.

I am grateful to the Instructor of ITI Satara for there continuous support from the very beginning of writing the book.

From this book, I consider myself blessed to have shared my thoughts on e-learning with you. I will not claim that this book is perfect, because considering the perfection, this book is an attempt and is in its infancy. They will be valuable for improvement if they are tested and suggested.

Manoj Dole
Dated 9/1/2019

Acknowledgements

The industrial training and theoretical examination system of our industrial training institutes and these changes have been accepted by the craft instructors and the trainees. Theoretical examinations conducted in your industrial training institutes are also conducted online. Since these examinations are of multiple choice MCQ method, the trainees will need to get more practice of such questions.

With all these considerations in mind, Mr. Manoj Madhukar, Director, Dole Crafts, Katari Industrial Training Institute, Satara, has done a thorough study and with his diligent work and added his keen intellect, according to the new annual system and NSQF-5 syllabus, e-book of Katari and other machine trades. -Book) and they have created mobile apps and blogs on theoretical topics to make training easier and have made all these educational materials available for download on the world famous websites Google Play Store, Amazon and Apple Book Store. Training has been made easier by creating a print version and using advanced techniques like QR Code.

All these educational materials will definitely be a guide for all the trainees for in-depth study and for the craft instructors and other concerned who are imparting vocational training.

Instrument Mechanic QR Code Images

Download App
Online Test Exam
ITI Books
AutoCAD CAM
JOB & Apprentice
Online Theory
Computer Course
Trading Course
CNC Course
MSCIT Course
Shopping Business
Internet Business
Web Designing
Online Services
Top Sportsmans
Indian Army
Freedom Fighters
Top Scientists
Social Reformers
Motivational Speaker
Top Richest People
Join WhatsApp Group
Join Facebook Group
Like Facebook Page
PAN / Adhar / Licence Passport

Fire extinguisher

Calliper

Hacksaw frame

Universal surface guage

Hammer

Centre punch

Bench vice

Files

Scraper

Surface Plate

Outside Micrometer

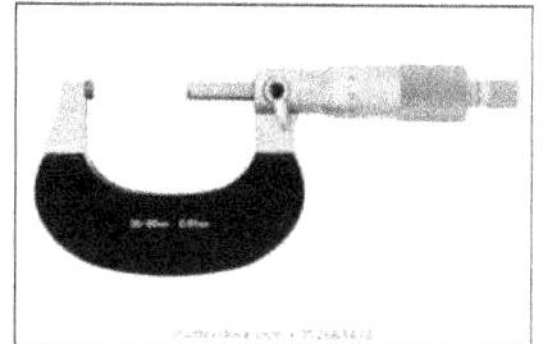 

Micrometer

Depth micrometer

Vernier Calliper

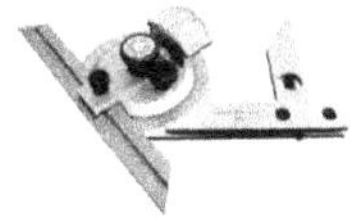 

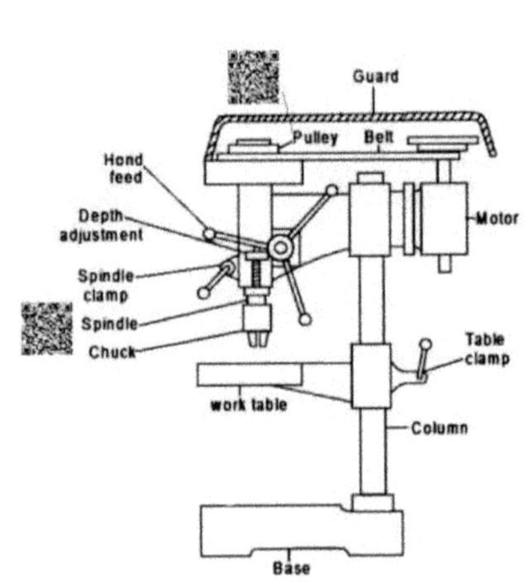

Piller Drilling Machine

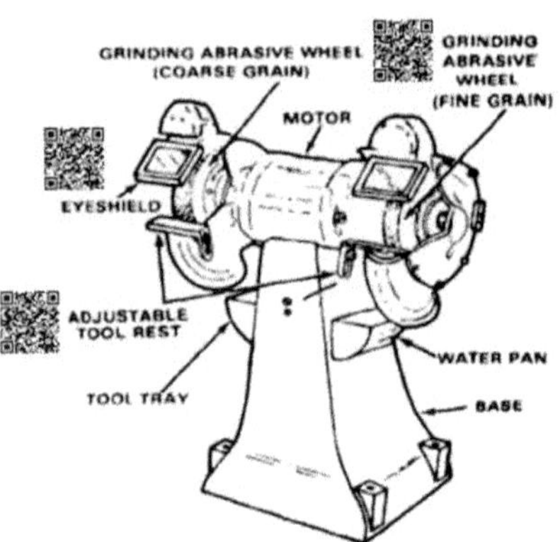

Pedastal Grinding Machine

ITI Book MCQ - Manoj Dole
www.itibook.com
battery
capacitor
cell
dynamometer
electromagnet
heater
inductance
magnet
www.itigov.blogspot.com   www.jobapprentices.blogspot.com   www.ititests.blogspot.com
www.itibook.com

15 ITI Book MCQ - Manoj Dole
www.itibook.com
megger
motor
multimeter
ohmmeter
resistores
star connected alternator
voltmeter ammeter
wattmeter
www.itigov.blogspot.com   www.jobapprentices.blogspot.com   www.ititests.blogspot.com
www.itibook.com

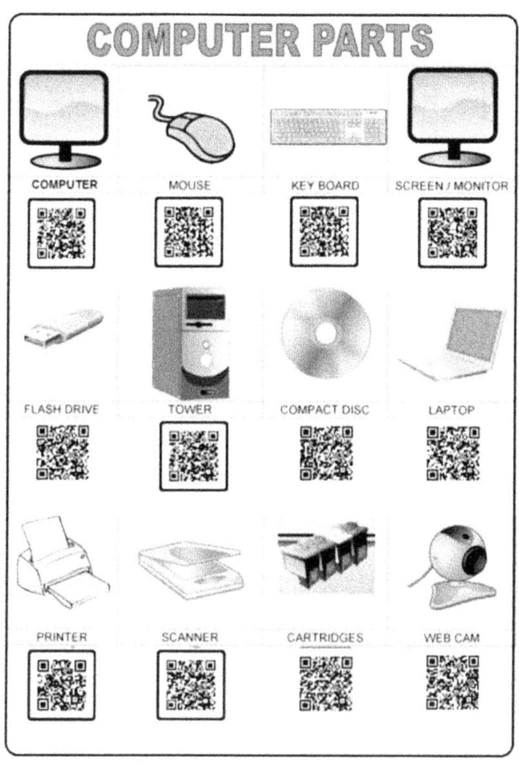
COMPUTER PARTS
COMPUTER
MOUSE
KEY BOARD
SCREEN / MONITOR
FLASH DRIVE
TOWER
COMPACT DISC
LAPTOP
PRINTER
SCANNER
CARTRIDGES
WEB CAM

COMPUTER PARTS
SPEAKER
HEADPHONES
SMARTPHONE
TABLET / I-PAD
MICROPHONE
WIRELESS ROUTER
MP3 PLAYER
JOYSTICK / GAME

CPU

Computer CPU
Hardware Components

Motherboard
Hardware Components

Excel Basic Functions

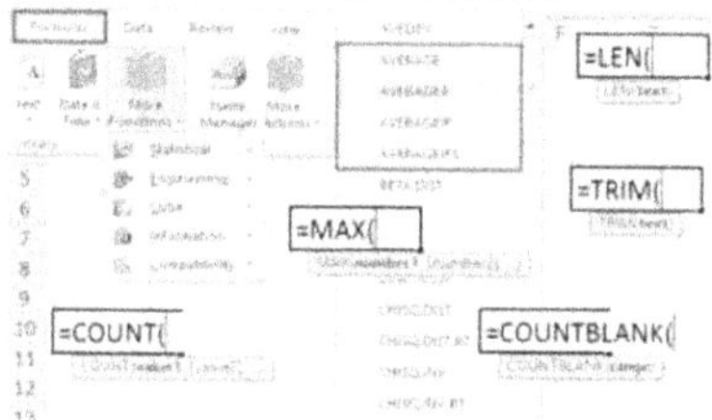

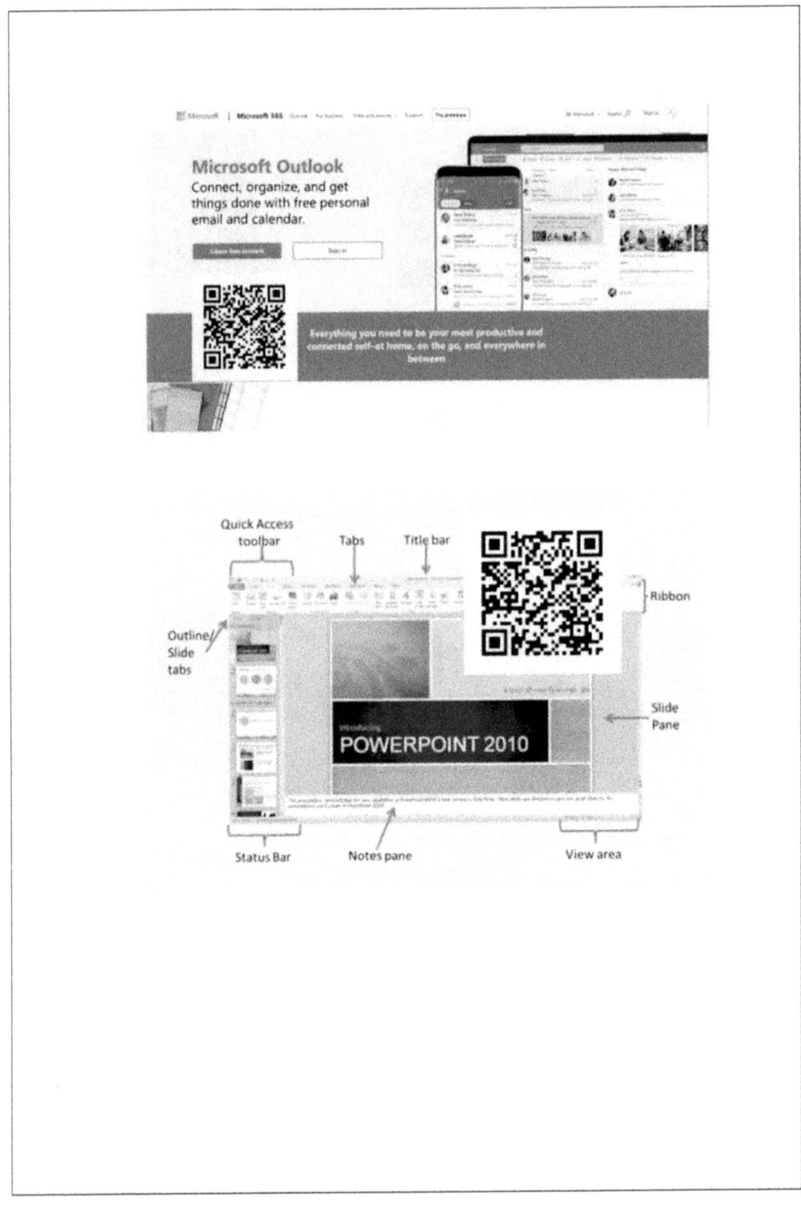
Microsoft Outlook
Connect, organize, and get things done with free personal email and calendar.
Everything you need to be your most productive and connected self-at home, on the go, and everywhere in between
Quick Access toolbar
Tabs
Title bar
Ribbon
Outline/ Slide tabs
Slide Pane
POWERPOINT 2010
Status Bar
Notes pane
View area

MS Paint
Microsoft
FEATURES OF
MS WORD
IN HINDI
WHAT IS MS WORD
HISTORY OF MS WORD
FEATURES OF MS WORD
Software Installation
Windows

CHAPTER TWO

Instrument Mechanic First Year MCQ

1] Which one is a workshop safety?

<u>A] Keep shop floor clean and free from grease, oil or other slippery materials</u>

B] Stop the machine before changing the speed

C] Don't use cracked or chipped tools

D] Don't try to stop a running machine with hand

2] In Personal Protect Equipment (PPE] HELMET is used to

<u>A] protect head</u>

B] Protect eyes

C] Protect hands

D] Protect ears

3] Which of the following belongs to general safety?

A Have a worker in good attitude

B] The work clean and clear

C] Concentrate on your work

<u>D] Keep the floor and gangways clean and clear</u>

4] While grinding, which is used to protect the eyes?

A] Dark green glass

B] Mask

C] Sun glasses

<u>D] Safety goggles</u>

5] Which of the following is done for machine safety?

<u>A] Check the oil level before starting the machine</u>

B] Do things in a methodical way

C] Keep the floor and gangways clean and clear

D] Don't use dies and scarves

6] In Personal Protect Equipment (PPE], 'sleeves' is used to protect ----------

A] Face

B] Eyes

C] Ears

<u>D] Hands</u>

7] ABC stands for --------------

A] Automatic Breathing Control

B] Automatic Blood Control

<u>C] Airway Breathing Circulation</u>

D] Automatic Blood Circulation

8] Fire & FIRE EXTINGUISHERS

Fire extinguisher

9] To put off"Class B" fire, the types of fire extinguisher used is ....

<u>A] dry power</u>

B] Carbon dioxide

C] Jet of water

D] Foam type

10] Which type of fire extinguisher is used to put off general fire?

<u>A] Water type Extinguisher</u>

B] Foam type Extinguisher

C] Dry chemical powder Extinguisher

D] Carbon dioxide (C02] Extinguisher

11] In case of bleeding, take treatment Of

D] cold 3" and rest

<u>A] spray cold water</u>

B] Bandage immediately -----.

B] Enquire about the accident thought treatment

12] in case of an accident, the victim should im

A] Asked to take rest

C] Attended immediately

D] leave him

13] First aid is given to an injured or ill person primarily....

A] Save life

B] Prevent further deterioration of the muff's

C] Give best possible comfort

D] All of these

14] Colour code for Bins for waste paper segregation is -----

A] blue Colour

B] Yellow Colour

C] Red Colour

D] Green Colour

15] In Japanese Seiko stands for --------------

A] Shine

B] Sort

C] Standardize

D] Sustain

16] Benefit of SS system is ------

A] Increase in productivity

B] Increase in quality

C] Reduction in wastage of time

D] All of these

17] Safety is -----------

A] nobody's business

B] every bodise business

C] Some bodies business

D] The organization business

18] For basic categories of safety signs are available The meaning of"prohibition" sign ----

A] shows it must not be done
B] Shows what must be done
C] Warns the hazard or danger
D] Gives information of safety provision

18] One micrometer (U] is equal to...
A] 0.1mm
B] 0.01mm
C] 0.001mm
D] 0.0001mm

19] The caliper meant for measuring the width of a slot is...
A] Odd leg caliper
B] Outside caliper
C] Jenny caliper
D] Inside calliper

Calliper

20] The size of the dividers are specified by the -----------
A] Total length of legs
B] Distance between the points when fully opened
C] Length of legs without points
D] distance between the pivot and the point

21] The instrument used to mark parallel lines, parallel to the datum edge is -
A] jenny caliper
B] Divider
C] Outside calliper
D] Inside calliper

22] Which one of the following is an indirect measuring tool?
A] Outside caliper
B] Vernier calliper
C] Steel rule

D] Outside micrometer

23] For cutting thin tubing, the most suitable pitch of the hacksaw blade is...

A] 1.8mm

B] 1.4mm

C] 1mm

D] 0.8mm

24] For cutting solid brass, the most suitable pitch of the hacksaw blade is...

A] 1.8mm

B] 1.4mm

C] 1mm

D] 0.8mm

Hacksaw frame

25] A new hacksaw blade after a few strokes becomes loose because of the...

A] Stretching of the blade

B] Wing-nut threads being worn out

C] Wrong pitch of the blade

D] Improper selection of the set of saws.

26] While cutting small diameter pipes, it is advisable to watch regularly and ensure that...

A] The cut is along the curved line

B] More saw teeth are in contract

C] The work is not overheated

D] Proper balancing of hacksaw is maintained

27] The vice clamps are used to...

A] Protect hard jaws

B] Clamp the work pieces rigidly

C] <u>Protect the finished surfaces</u>

D] Prevent the movable jaw being filed

28] The reference surface during marking is provided by the...

A] Surface gauge

B] Workpiece

C] Drawing of the work

D] <u>Marking table surface</u>

29] The size of an engineer's vice is specified by the...

A] Length of the movable jaw

B] <u>Width of the jaws</u>

C] Height of the vice

D] Maximum opening of the jaws

30] The part of the universal surface gauge which helps to draw a parallel line along a datum edge is the..

A] Rocker arm

B] Snug

C] Fine adjustment screw

D] <u>Guide pins</u>

Universal surface guage

31] Scribers are made of...

A] Mild steel

B] <u>High carbon steel</u>

C] Brass

D] Cast iron

32] Portion of the hammer used for fixing the handle is...

A] Face

B] Peen

C] Cheek

D] <u>Eye hole</u>

33] Weight of the hammer for the marking purpose is...

A] <u>250g</u>

B] 500g

C] 1 kg

D] 2 kgs

Hammer

34] The size of the dividers are specified by the...

A] Total length of the legs

B] Distance between the points when fully opened

C] Length of legs without the points

D] <u>Distance between the pivot and the point</u>

35] The included angle of the groove of 'V' block is always....

A] 45°

B] 60°

C] 90°

D] <u>120°</u>

36] 'V' blocks are available in grades of...

A] <u>A & B</u>

B] A,B & C

C] 1,2 & 3

D] 1 & 2

37] 'V' blocks of grade 'B' are made of

A] <u>Cast iron</u>

B] Mild steel

C] Steel

D] Cast steel

38] Name the punch used to locate the centre.

A] Prick punch 30°

B] Prick punch 60°

C] <u>Centre punch</u>

D] Dot punch

Centre punch

39] The point angle of centre punch is --------

A] 30°

B] 50°

c] <u>900</u>

D] 1200

40] Punches are used for forming ---------of any shape

A] <u>Holes</u>

B] Mining

C] Knurling

D] Reaming

41] Generally the length of the handle of the vice is ----------

A] 1.5 times the normal size of the vice

B] <u>2.5 times the normal size of the vice</u>

C] 3.5 times the normal size of the vice

D] 4.5 times the normal size of the vice

Bench vice

42] Bench vice spindle is made of ....

A] mild steel

B] Cast iron

C] Tool steel

D] Bronze

43] The convexity of files helps...

A] To file concave surfaces

B] To file convex surfaces

C] To prevent rounding of edges of work

D] The file to become straight when pressure is applied

Files

44] Which file used for filling wood, leather and other soft material? .

A] Single cut file

B] Double cut file

c] Rasp cut file

D] Curved cut file

45] File used is used for ------------

A] Cleaning the work piece

C] Renewing the file teeth
B] <u>cleaning the file teeth</u>
D] Cleaning the chips
46] File card is used to --------
A] Clean the work piece
C] Renew the file teeth
B] <u>Clean the file teeth</u>
47] The point angle of scriber is -----------
A] 30°
B] 60°
C] 5° to 10°
D] <u>12° to 15°</u>
48] The cutting angle for chipping cast iron is...
A] 37.5°
B] 55°
C] <u>60°</u>
D] 90°

49] The chisel will dig into the material when...
A] The rake angle is more
B] The clearance angle is too low
C] <u>The angle of inclination is more</u>
D] The angle of inclination is too low
50] A slight convexity is given to the cutting edge to...
A] Cut curved surfaces
B] Cut sharp corners
C] <u>Prevent digging of the ends</u>
D] Allow the lubricant to enter
51] Surface plates are made of...
A] High grade cast steel
B] <u>Fine-grained cast iron</u>
C] Alloy steels

D] Wrought iron

52] Surface plates are specified by their length and breadth & are in

A] decimetre

B] Cubic meter

C] <u>Cylindrical</u>

53] Ribs are given on the unmachined portion of the angle plate for...

A] Easy handling

B] Convenience in manufacturing

C] Clamping while setting on machines

D] <u>Rigidity and to prevent distortion</u>

54] The slots on the angle plate are given for...

A] Reducing weight

B] Aligning the work

C] Lifting using hooks

D] <u>Accommodating bolts</u>.

55] The size of the angle plates is stated by...

A] Weight

B] Length

C] Length x width

D] <u>Size number</u>

56] for high speed parting off work on material like cemented carbide Is'

A] Do all machine

B] Cutting off machine

C] <u>Heavy duty power saw</u>

D] Mining machine sitting saw

57] Gun metal is an alloy of copper, ------------

A] <u>tin and zinc</u>

B] Lead and zinc

C] Zinc and nickel

D] Lead and nickel

58] Cast iron is used for manufacturing machine beds because -------

A] it can resist more compressive stress
B] it is heavy in weight
C] It is cheaper metal
D] It is a brittle metal

59] Accuracy or least count of a metric outside micrometric is ---------
A] 0-1 mm
B] 0.01 mm
C] 0.001 mm
D] 0.02 mm

60] 1000 microns means -----
A] 1 mm
B] 1 m
C] 1000 mm
D] 10 cm

61] in a metric micrometer, a complete revolution of thimble advances -----------
A] 0.01 mm
B] 0.25 mm
C] 0.50 mm
D] 1.00mm

Micrometer

62] Ratchet Stop in the micrometer helps to ------------

A] Control the pressure

B] lock the spindle

C] Adjust the zero error

D] Hold the work piece

63] 1000 micron means ------------

A] 1 mm

B] 1 m

C] 1000 mm

D] 10 cm

64] What is the zero reading of a 50-75 mm outside micrometer?

A] 0.000 mm

B] 0.01 mm

C] 25.00 mm

D] 50.00 mm

65] The value of the smallest division on sleeve of a metric outside micrometer is -----

A] 0.50 mm

B] 1.00 mm

C] 1.50 mm

D] 2.00 mm

66] Ratchet stop in the micrometer helps to ---------

A] control the pressure

B] Lock the spindle

C] Adjust the zero error

D] Hold the work piece

67] Least count of depth micrometer is

A] 0.5 mm

B] 0.2 mm

C] 0.001 mm

D] 0.01 mm

Depth micrometer

68] The least count of vernier calliper is (main scale = 49 division, vernier scale = 50 division]

A] 0.1 mm

B] 0.01 mm

C] 0.001 mm

D] 0.02 mm

Vernier Calliper

69] The type of measurement made by using a Vernier Calliper is -------

A] Direct measurement

B] Indirect measurement

C] 90"] (a] 81 (b]

D] None of these

70] The least count of a vernier bevel protractor is...

A] 1"

B] 5'

C] 1∘

D] 5∘

71] The part of a vernier bevel protractor which is normally used as a reference base for measuring angles is the...

A] Blade

B] <u>Stock</u>

C] Disc

C] Main scale

Vernier bevel protractor

72] The part of a vernier bevel protector on which main scale divisions are marked is the...

A] Stock

B] Dial

C] <u>Disc</u>

D] Adjustable blade

73] The part of a bevel protractor, which comes in contact with the inclined surface while measuring is the...

A] <u>Blade</u>

B] Stock

C] Disc

D] Dial

74] The value of each division of the main scale of a vernier bevel protractor is...

A] 5'

B] <u>1°</u>

C] 5°

D]10°

75] The value of each division of the vernier scale of a bevel protractor is...

A] 1°

B] 1∘5'
C] <u>1∘55'</u>
D] 5'
76] The taper shank drills are held on the machine by means of...
A] Chucks
B] <u>Sleeves</u>
C] Drift
D] Vice

77] Drill chucks are fitted on the drilling machine spindle by means of a...
A] Knurled ring
B] <u>Arbor</u>
C] Drift
D] Pinion and key
78] The Morse taper provided on drills ranges between...
A] <u>MT 1 to MT 5</u>
B] MT 1 to MT 4
C] MT 0 to MT 5
D] MT 0 to MT 4
79] A drift is used for...
A] Drawing a drill location
B] Fixing chuck on the machine spindle
C] Removing a broken drill from the work
D] <u>Removing the drill from the machine spindle</u>
80] When the taper shank of the drill is larger than the machine spindle, the device to hold the drill is a...
A] Drill sleeve
B] <u>Taper socket</u>
C] Drill drift
D] Chuck and key
81] The suitable cutting fluid for drilling mild steel in a drilling machine is...

A] Synthetic soluble oil

B] Neat oil

C] Distilled water

D] <u>Soluble oil</u>

82] A special feature of the radial drilling machine is...

A] It can be used for drilling with a H.S.S. drill

B] Table can be moved and set at any position

C] A variety of speeds is available

D] <u>The spindle can be brought to any position</u>

83] The point angle of drills depends on...

A] The size of the drill

B] The type of machine

C] <u>The material of the work</u>

D] The RPM of the drill

84] The point angle for a standard drill is...

A] 60°

B] 108°

C] <u>118°</u>

D] 135°

85] The helical angle determines the...

A] Cutting angle

B] Chew angle

C] <u>Rake angle</u>

D] Lip angle

86] The clearance angle of the drill is between...

A] 3° to 5°

B] <u>8° to 12°</u>

C] 12° to 20°
D] 15° to 20°
87] In a remote place (no electricity available] a rail track is to be drilled. Choose the right drilling machine
A] Radial drilling machine
B] Pillar drilling machine
C] <u>Ratchet drilling machine</u>
D] Sensitive drilling Machine

Drilling
88] A drilling machine used by a carpenter for cabinet making is a...
A] Ratchet drilling machine
B] Radial drilling machine
C] <u>Breast drilling machine</u>
D] Sensitive drilling machine
89] Which one of the following drilling machines is used for drilling holes where electricity is not available?
A] Bench drilling machine
B] Pillar drilling machine
C] Redial drilling machine
D] <u>Ratchet drilling machine</u>
90] Which one of the following drilling machine is used for heavy duty work?
A] Bench drilling machine
B] Pillar drilling machine
C] <u>Radial drilling machine</u>
D] Electric hand drilling machine
91] Drill chuck are held on the machine spindle by means of ------
A] <u>arbor</u>
B] Drift

C] draw-in bar

D] Chuck nut

92] Different speeds are obtained in a sensitive bench drilling machine by ----

A] Belt pulley mechanism

B] Hydraulic mechanism

C] Rack and Pinion mechanism

D] Cam and follower mechanism

176] 50 metric coarse thread is designated as M12 x 125 What does '12' indicate?

A] Major diameter

B] Root diameter

C] Pitch diameter

D] Blank diameter

179] the top surface joining the two sides of adjacent thread is called

A] Crest

B] Root

C] Flank

D] Thread is angle

Thread

180] The included angle of the ISO metric thread is --------

A] 27 1 /2°

B] 30°

C] 55°

D] 60°

181] Which one of the following screw thread forms has an included angle of 55° between the flanks of threads?

A] B. A. Thread

B] Acme thread

C] Buttress threads

D] Knuckle thread

182] Which one of the following is used only for finishing and maintaining correct form of thread?

A] Tap

B] Threading tool

C] Threading chaser

D] Tipped tool

183] The angle 0f lS thread (V shaped] is ----------

A] 29°

B] 47 1/4°

C] 50°

D] 60

184] ln which of the following methods, only external threads are made --------

A] Form tool mEthOd

B] Compound rest method

C] Tailstock offset method

D] Taper turning attachment method.

185] The surface joining the crest and the root of a thread is known as ----

A] Flank

B] Shank

C] Pitch surface

D] All Of these

186] Pitch of a two start thread is 4 mm. Then the lead of the thread is given by -----

A] 4mm

B] 2mm

C] 8mm

D] 6mm

188] A die in which more than one cutting operation is per formed in one stroke

A] Piercing die

B] Progressive die

C] Combination die

D] Compound die

189] A die in which cutting and non cutting operations are carried out per stroke.

A] Piercing die

B] Progressive die

C] <u>Combination die</u>

D] Compound die

Tap Die

190] A die in which two or more sequential operations are performed at two or more stations upon the work.

A] Piercing die

B] <u>Progressive die</u>

C] Combination die

D] Compound die

191] A die in which the shape of the punch and die are directly reproduced in the metal with little or no metal flow.

A] Progressive die

B] Combination die

C] Compound die

D] <u>Forming die</u>

192] The die used for producing any shape of holes.

A] <u>Piercing die</u>

B] Progressive die

C] Combination die

D] Compound die

193] Abrasives are classifications into.............

A] <u>Two types</u>

B] Three types

c] One types

D] Four types

194] Grinding wheels made out of----------------- abrasive are most common because of its free and cool cutting action.

A] Aluminium oxide

B] Silicon oxide

C] Ammonium oxide

D] Carbide.

195] Which among the following abrasive is mostly used for cutting off wheels for cutting non metallic materials?

A] Aluminium oxide

B] Silicon carbide

C] Diamond

D] None of above

196] Which abrasive particle is used for grinding tungsten carbide tool insert?

A] Silicon carbide

B] A|203

C] Diamond

D] Corundum

197] Which of the following is the natural abrasive?

A] Aluminium oxide

B] Silicon

C] Boron carbide

D] Corundum

198] Which of the following is the manufactured abrasive?

A] Corundum.

B] Quartz

C] Silicon

D] Emery

199] Which abrasive particle is used for grinding steel fittings?

A] Silicon carbide

B] Aluminium oxide

C] Diamond.

D] boron oxide

200] What kind of abrasive cut of wheel should be used to cut concrete stone and masonry?

A] Silicon

B] Al203

C] Diamond grit

D] Glass

201] Aluminium oxide wheel is used for grinding ------------

A] cast iron

B] Cemented carbide.

C] HSS '

D] ceramic

202] The bond of diamond wheel suitable for offhand grinding of the tipped tool is ....

A] Resinoid

B] Vitrified

C] Shellac

D] Metal

Grinding Wheel

203] Which among the following bonds, is used commonly?

A] Vitrified bond '

B] Rubber bond

C] Shellac bond

D] Silicate bond

204] The symbol conventionally used for resinoid .bond is ~~~~~~~~

A] v

B] R f

C] B

D] E

205] In grinding practice the term "grade of wheel" refers to ---------'

A] Hardness of the abrasive used

B] Strength of the bond of the wheel

C] Finish 0f the Wheel

D] Hardness of the work pieces

206] Which bond is used in cut of wheels?

A] Rubber

B] Vitrified

C] Resirjoid

D] Shellac

207] Hardness of grinding wheel is determine by ----------

A] the resistance exerted. by the bond against grinding Stress

B] Hardness of abrasive grains

C] Hardness of bond

D] Ability to penetration

208] When it is required to run a Grinding wheel safely at very high speed, which bond should be used? "

A] Vitrified

B] Shellac

C] Silicate

D] resinoid' and rubber

209] in surface grinding what is the suitable range of grain size of the grinding wheel for general purpose surface grinding?

A] 20 to 36

B] 46 to 60

C] 80 to 120

D] 150 to 300

210] AS per Indian Standard, the grain '46'.comes under the group of «w. -----

A] Coarse

B] Medium

C] Fine

D] Very fine

211] The grit size of the abrasives used in the grinding wheel is usually specified by ----------

A] Hardness number

B] A size of wheel

C] Softness or hardness of the abrasive

D] Mesh number

212] Bench grinder are used for ....

A] Heavy duty work

B] Heavy and light duty work

C] Light duty work

D] Lather work

213] Bench Grinders are fitted on a ....

A] Base

B] Table.

C] Wheel guards

D] Conveyor

214] Which of the following statement is correct?'

A] Gauges are used to check the size

B] Template are used to chuck-the size

C] Gauges are used to measure the size

D] Gauges are used to check shape of component

215] At what standard temperature are the gauges kept in the section?

A] 100 C

B] 20° C

C] 100 F

D] 20° F

216] Which grade of slip gauge is generally used in workshop?

A] Grade 0

B] Grade l

C] Grade H

D] Grade 0

Slip gauge

217] As per Indian Standards a special set gauge is used consisting of

A].81 Pieces

B] 112 Pieces

C] 120 Pieces

D] 130 Pieces

218] The accuracy of reference gauge is

A] 0.05 mm

B] 0.01 mm

C] 0.001 .

D] 0.0001 mm

219] ln case of ant burr on slip gauge, it should be removed by

A] Filling

B] Lapping

C] Scraping

D] Grinding

220] Hardness of slip gauge should be?

A] More than 63 HRC

B] 58 HRC

C] 55 HRC

D] 50 HRC

221]------------- Slip gauge is used for Checking component within an accuracy of 0.01 mm.

A] Workshop gauge

B] Inspection gauge

C] Reference gauge

D] Ring gauge

222], ------------is used for checking accuracy of precision instrument.

A] Gauge block

B] Fader gauge

C] Sine bar

D] Plug gauge

223] Slip gauge are Cleaned before using to ensure accuracy. What medium will you use for this purpose.

A] Oil

B] Thinner

C] Carbon tetrachloride/ White petrol

D] Turpentine oil

Q 18. PVC plug is used to _______________.

A). Connect pipes of varying diameters

B). Connect two pipe lines

C). Seal pipes of small diameter

D). Seal ends of pipe line

Q 19. Which pipe fitting allows contents of two pipes to flow together into one pipe?

A). Lateral

B). Cross

C). Elbow

D). Return bend

Q 20. The choice of method for tube bending depends upon __________.

A). Diameter of tube

B). Wall thickness of tube

C). Minimum bend radius required

D). All of these

Q 21. What is the method of tube bending shown in figure given below?

A) Rotary draw bending

B) Ram bending

C) Compression bending

D) Roll bending

Q 22. Which of these statements is NOT true?

A). Manholes are provided in sewer pipes at suitable intervals

B).. Catch basins are generally provided in sewers for carrying drainage discharge

C). Inlets are generally provided in all sewers

D). None of these

Q 23. The asbestos cement pipes are generally laid ___________.

A). Horizontally

B). Vertically

C). At an angle of 30 degrees

D). At an angle of 60 degrees

Q 24. Chlorination of water is done for removal of ___________.

A). Bacterias

B). Suspended solids

C). Sediments

D). Hardness

Q 25. Removal of grease and oil from sewage is called _________.

A). Screening

B). Filtering

C). Skimming

D). Bypassing

1. The S.I. unit of power is

(a) Henry

(b) coulomb

(c) watt

(d) watt-hour

2. Electric pressure is also called

(a) resistance

(b) power

(c) <u>voltage</u>

(d) energy

3. The substances which have a large number of free electrons and offer a low
resistance are called

(a) insulators

(b) inductors

(c) semi-conductors

(d) <u>conductors</u>

4. Out of the following which is not a poor conductor ?

(a) Cast iron

(b) <u>Copper</u>

(c) Carbon

(d) Tungsten

5. Out of the following which is an insulating material ?

(a) Copper

(b) Gold

(c) Silver

(d) <u>Paper</u>

6. The property of a conductor due to which it passes current is called

(a) resistance

(b) reluctance

(c) <u>conductance</u>

(d) inductance

7. Conductance is reciprocal of

(a) <u>resistance</u>

(b) inductance

(c) reluctance

(d) capacitance

8. The resistance of a conductor varies inversely as

(a) length

(b) <u>area of cross-section</u>

(c) temperature

(d) resistivity

9. With rise in temperature the resistance of pure metals

(a) increases

(b) decreases

(c) first increases and then decreases

(d) remains constant

10. With rise in temperature the resistance of semi-conductors

(a) decreases

(b) increases

(c) first increases and then decreases

(d) remains constant

11. The resistance of a copper wire 200 m long is 21 Q. If its thickness (diameter)

is 0.44 mm, its specific resistance is around

(a) 1.2 x 10~8 Q-m

(b) 1.4 x 10~8 Q-m

(c) 1.6 x 10""8 Q-m

(d) 1.8 x 10"8 Q-m

13. An instrument which detects electric current is known as

(a) voltmeter

(b) rheostat

(c) wattmeter

(d) galvanometer

14. In a circuit a 33 Q resistor carries a current of 2 A. The voltage across the resistor is

(a) 33 V

(b) 66 v

(c) 80 V

(d) 132 V

15. A light bulb draws 300 mA when the voltage across it is 240 V. The resistance of the light bulb is

(a) 400 Q

(b) 600 Q

(c) 800 Q

(d) 1000 Q

16. The resistance of a parallel circuit consisting of two branches is 12 ohms. If the resistance of one branch is 18 ohms, what is the resistance of the other ?

(a) 18 Q

(b) <u>36 Q</u>

(c) 48 Q

(d) 64 Q

17. Four wires of same material, the same cross-sectional area and the same length when connected in parallel give a resistance of 0.25 Q. If the same four wires are connected is series the effective resistance will be

(a) 1 Q

(b) 2 Q

(c) 3 Q

(d) <u>4 Q</u>

18. A current of 16 amperes divides between two branches in parallel of resistances 8 ohms and 12 ohms respectively. The current in each branch is

(a) 6.4 A, 6.9 A

(b) <u>6.4 A, 9.6 A</u>

(c) 4.6 A, 6.9 A

(d) 4.6 A, 9.6 A

19. Current velocity through a copper conductor is

(a) the same as propagation velocity of electric energy

(b) independent of current strength

(c) <u>of the order of a few ^.s/m</u>

(d) nearly 3 x 108 m/s

20. Which of the following material has nearly zero temperature co-efficient of resistance?

(a) <u>Manganin</u>

(b) Porcelain

(c) Carbon

(d) Copper

21. You have to replace 1500 Q resistor in radio. You have no 1500 Q resistor but have several 1000 Q ones which you would connect

(a) two in parallel

(b) <u>two in parallel and one in series</u>

(c) three in parallel

(d) three in series

22. Two resistors are said to be connected in series when

(a) <u>same current passes in turn through both</u>

(b) both carry the same value of current

(c) total current equals the sum of branch currents

(d) sum of IR drops equals the applied e.m.f.

23. Which of the following statement is true both for a series and a parallel D.C. circuit?

(a) Elements have individual currents

(b) Currents are additive

(c) Voltages are additive

(d) <u>Power are additive</u>

24. Which of the following materials has a negative temperature co-efficient of resistance?

(a) Copper

(b) Aluminum

(c) <u>Carbon</u>

(d) Brass

25. Ohm's law is not applicable to

(a) <u>vacuum tubes</u>

(b) carbon resistors

(c) high voltage circuits

(d) circuits with low current densities

26. Which is the best conductor of electricity ?

(a) Iron

(b) <u>Silver</u>

(c) Copper

(d) Carbon

27. For which of the following 'ampere second' could be the unit ?

(a) Reluctance

(b) <u>Charge</u>

(c) Power

(d) Energy

28. All of the following are equivalent to watt except

(a) (amperes) ohm

(b) joules/sec.

(c) amperes x volts

(d) <u>amperes/volt</u>

29. A resistance having rating 10 ohms, 10 W is likely to be a

(a) metallic resistor

(b) carbon resistor

(c) <u>wire wound resistor</u>

(d) variable resistor

30. Which one of the following does not have negative temperature co-efficient ?
(a) <u>Aluminium</u>
(b) Paper
(c) Rubber
(d) Mica

31. Varistors are
(a) insulators
(6) <u>non-linear resistors</u>
(c) carbon resistors
(d) resistors with zero temperature coefficient

32. Insulating materials have the function of
(a) preventing a short circuit between conducting wires
(b) <u>preventing an open circuit between the voltage source and the load</u>
(c) conducting very large currents
(d) storing very high currents

33. The rating of a fuse wire is always expressed in
(a) ampere-hours
(b) ampere-volts
(c) kWh
(d) <u>amperes</u>

34. The minimum charge on an ion is
(a) equal to the atomic number of the atom
(b) <u>equal to the charge of an electron</u>
(c) equal to the charge of the number of electrons in an atom (#) zero

35. In a series circuit with unequal resistances
(a) the highest resistance has the most of the current through it
(b) the lowest resistance has the highest voltage drop
(c) the lowest resistance has the highest current
(d) <u>the highest resistance has the highest voltage drop</u>

36. The filament of an electric bulb is made of
(a) carbon
(b) aluminium
(c) tungsten
(d) nickel

37. A 3 Q resistor having 2 A current will dissipate the power of
(a) 2 watts
(b) 4 watts

(c) <u>6 watts</u>

(d) 8 watts

38. Which of the following statement is true?

(a) A galvanometer with low resistance in parallel is a voltmeter

(b) A galvanometer with high resistance in parallel is a voltmeter

(c) <u>A galvanometer resistance in series is an ammeter with low</u>

(d) A galvanometer with high resistance in series is an ammeter

39. The resistance of a few meters of wire conductor in closed electrical circuit is

(a) <u>practically zero</u>

(b) low

(c) high

(d) very high

40. If a parallel circuit is opened in the main line, the current

(a) increases in the branch of the lowest resistance

(b) increases in each branch

(c) <u>is zero in all branches</u>

(d) is zero in the highest resistive branch

41. If a wire conductor of 0.2 ohm resistance is doubled in length, its resistance becomes

(a) <u>0.4 ohm</u>

(b) 0.6 ohm

(c) 0.8 ohm

(d) 1.0 ohm

42. Three 60 W bulbs are in parallel across the 60 V power line. If one bulb burns open

(a) there will be heavy current in the main line

(b) rest of the two bulbs will not light

(c) all three bulbs will light

(d) <u>the other two bulbs will light</u>

43. The four bulbs of 40 W each are connected in series swift a battery across them, which of the following statement is true ?

(a) <u>The current through each bulb in same</u>

(b) The voltage across each bulb is not same

(c) The power dissipation in each bulb is not same

(d) None of the above

44. Two resistances Rl and Ri are connected in series across the voltage source where Rl>Ri. The largest drop will be across

(a) Rl
(b) Ri
(c) either Rl or Ri
(d) none of them

46. A closed switch has a resistance of
(a) zero
(b) about 50 ohms
(c) about 500 ohms
(d) infinity

47. The hot resistance of the bulb's filament is higher than its cold resistance because the temperature co-efficient of the filament is
(a) zero
(b) negative
(c) positive
(d) about 2 ohms per degree

49. The insulation on a current carrying conductor is provided
(a) to prevent leakage of current
(b) to prevent shock
(c) both of above factors
(d) none of above factors

50. The thickness of insulation provided on the conductor depends on
(a) the magnitude of voltage on the conductor
(b) the magnitude of current flowing through it
(c) both (a) and (b)
(d) none of the above

51. Which of the following quantities remain the same in all parts of a series circuit ?
(a) Voltage
(b) Current
(c) Power
(d) Resistance

52. A 40 W bulb is connected in series with a room heater. If now 40 W bulb is replaced by 100 W bulb, the heater output will
(a) decrease
(b) increase
(c) remain same
(d) heater will burn out

53. In an electric kettle water boils in 10 m minutes. It is required to boil the boiler in 15 minutes, using same supply mains

(a) <u>length of heating element should be decreased</u>

(b) length of heating element should be increased

(c) length of heating element has no effect on heating if water

(d) none of the above

54. An electric filament bulb can be worked from

(a) D.C. supply only

(b) A.C. supply only

(c) Battery supply only

(d) <u>All above</u>

55. Resistance of a tungsten lamp as applied voltage increases

(a) decreases

(b) <u>increases</u>

(c) remains same

(d) none of the above

56. Electric current passing through the circuit produces

(a) magnetic effect

(b) luminous effect

(c) <u>thermal effect</u>

(d) chemical effect

(e) all above effects

57. Resistance of a material always decreases if

(a) temperature of material is decreased

(6) temperature of material is increased

(c) number of free electrons available become more

(d) none of the above is correct

58. If the efficiency of a machine is to be high, what should be low ?

(a) Input power

(b) <u>Losses</u>

(c) True component of power

(d) kWh consumed

(e) Ratio of output to input

59. When electric current passes through a metallic conductor, its temperature rises. This is due to

(a) <u>collisions between conduction electrons and atoms</u>

(b) the release of conduction electrons from parent atoms

(c) mutual collisions between metal atoms

(d) mutual collisions between conducting electrons

60. Two bulbs of 500 W and 200 W rated at 250 V will have resistance ratio as

(a) 4 : 25

(b) 25 : 4

(c) 2 : 5

(d) 5 : 2

61. A glass rod when rubbed with silk cloth is charged because

(a) it takes in proton

(b) its atoms are removed

(c) it gives away electrons

(d) it gives away positive charge

62. Whether circuit may be AC. or D.C. one, following is most effective in

reducing the magnitude of the current.

(a) Reactor

(b) Capacitor

(c) Inductor

(d) Resistor

63. It becomes more difficult to remove

(a) any electron from the orbit

(6) first electron from the orbit

(c) second electron from the orbit

(d) third electron from the orbit

64. When one leg of parallel circuit is opened out the total current will

(a) reduce

(b) increase

(c) decrease

(d) become zero

65. In a lamp load when more than one lamp are switched on the total resistance

of the load

(a) increases

(b) decreases

(c) remains same

(d) none of the above

66. Two lamps 100 W and 40 W are connected in series across 230 V (alternating).

Which of the following statement is correct ?

(a) 100 W lamp will glow brighter

(b) <u>40 W lamp will glow brighter</u>

(c) Both lamps will glow equally bright

(d) 40 W lamp will fuse

67. Resistance of 220 V, 100 W lamp will be

(a) 4.84 Q

(b) 48.4 Q

(c) <u>484 ft</u>

(d) 4840 Q

68. In the case of direct current

(a) <u>magnitude and direction of current remains constant</u>

(b) magnitude and direction of current changes with time

(c) magnitude of current changes with time

(d) magnitude of current remains constant

69. When electric current passes through a bucket full of water, lot of bubbling is

observed. This suggests that the type of supply is

(a) A.C.

(b) <u>D.C.</u>

(c) any of above two

(d) none of the above

70. Resistance of carbon filament lamp as the applied voltage increases.

(a) increases

(b) <u>decreases</u>

(c) remains same

(d) none of the above

71. Bulbs in street lighting are all connected in

(a) <u>parallel</u>

(b) series

(c) series-parallel

(d) end-to-end

72. For testing appliances, the wattage of test lamp should be

(a) very low

(b) low

(c) <u>high</u>

(d) any value

73. Switching of a lamp in house produces noise in the radio. This is because switching operation produces

(a) arcs across separating contacts

(b) mechanical noise of high intensity

(c) both mechanical noise and arc between contacts

(d) none of the above

74. Sparking occurs when a load is switched off because the circuit has high

(a) resistance

(b) inductance

(c) capacitance

(d) impedance

75. Copper wire of certain length and resistance is drawn out to three times its

length without change in volume, the new resistance of wire becomes

(a) 1/9 times

(b) 3 times

(c) 9 times

(d) unchanged

76. When resistance element of a heater fuses and then we reconnect it after removing a portion of it, the power of the heater will

(a) decrease

(b) increase

(c) remain constant

(d) none of the above

77. A field of force can exist only between

(a) two molecules

(b) two ions

(c) two atoms

(d) two metal particles

78. A substance whose molecules consist of dissimilar atoms is called

(a) semi-conductor

(b) super-conducto

(c) compound

(d) insulator

79. International ohm is defined in terms of the resistance of

(a) a column of mercury

(b) a cube of carbon

(c) a cube of copper

(d) the unit length of wire

80. Three identical resistors are first connected in parallel and then in series.

The resultant resistance of the first combination to the second will be

(a) 9 times

(b) <u>1/9 times</u>

(c) 1/3 times

(d) 3 times

91. Which method can be used for absolute measurement of resistances ?

(a) Lorentz method

(b) Releigh method

(c) Ohm's law method

(d) <u>Wheatstone bridge method</u>

92. Three 6 ohm resistors are connected to form a triangle. What is the resistance between any two corners ?

(a) 3/2 Q

(b 6 Q

(c) <u>4 Q</u>

(d) 8/3 Q

93. Ohm's law is not applicable to

(a) <u>semi-conductors</u>

(b) D.C. circuits

(c) small resistors

(d) high currents

94. Two copper conductors have equal length. The cross-sectional area of one conductor is four times that of the other. If the conductor having smaller crosssectional area has a resistance of 40 ohms the resistance of other conductor will be

(a) 160 ohms

(b) 80 ohms

(c) 20 ohms

(d) <u>10 ohms</u>

95. A nichrome wire used as a heater coil has the resistance of 2 £2/m. For a heater of 1 kW at 200 V, the length of wire required will be

(a) <u>80 m</u>

(b) 60 m

(c) 40 m

(d) 20 m

96. Temperature co-efficient of resistance is expressed in terms of

(a) ohms/°C

(b) mhos/ohm°C

(c) <u>ohms/ohm°C</u>

98. When current flows through heater coil it glows but supply wiring does not glow because

(a) current through supply line flows at slower speed

(b) supply wiring is covered with insulation layer

(c) <u>resistance of heater coil is more than the supply wires</u>

(d) supply wires are made of superior material

99. The condition for the validity under Ohm's law is that

(a) <u>resistance must be uniform</u>

(b) current should be proportional to the size of the resistance

(c) resistance must be wire wound type

(d) temperature at positive end should be more than the temperature at negative end

100. Which of the following statement is correct ?

(a) <u>A semi-conductor is a material whose conductivity is same as between that of a conductor and an insulator</u>

(b) A semi-conductor is a material which has conductivity having average value of conductivity of metal and insulator

(c) A semi-conductor is one which con¬ducts only half of the applied voltage

(d) A semi-conductor is a material made of alternate layers of conducting material and insulator

101. A rheostat differs from potentiometer in the respect that it

(a) has lower wattage rating

(b) <u>has higher wattage rating</u>

(c) has large number of turns

(d) offers large number of tapping

102. The weight of an aluminium conductor as compared to a copper conductor of identical cross-section, for the same electrical resistance, is

(a) <u>50%</u>

(b) 60%

(c) 100%

(d) 150%

103. An open resistor, when checked with an ohm-meter reads
(a) zero
(b) <u>infinite</u>
(c) high but within tolerance
(d) low but not zero
104. are the materials having electrical conductivity much less than most of the metals but much greater than that of typical insulators.
(a) Varistors
(b) Thermistor
(c) <u>Semi-conductors</u>
(d) Variable resistors
105. All good conductors have high
(a) <u>conductance</u>
(b) resistance
(c) reluctance
(d) thermal conductivity
106. Voltage dependent resistors are usually made from
(a) charcoal
(b) silicon carbide
(c) <u>nichrome</u>
(d) graphite
107. Voltage dependent resistors are used
(a) for inductive circuits
(b) <u>to supress surges</u>
(c) as heating elements
(d) as current stabilizers
108. The ratio of mass of proton to that of electron is nearly
(a) <u>1840</u>
(b) 1840
(c) 30
(d) 4
109. The number of electrons in the outer most orbit of carbon atom is
(a) 3
(b) <u>4</u>
(c) 6
(d) 7
110. With three resistances connected in parallel, if each dissipates 20 W the total power supplied by the voltage source equals

(a) 10 W

(b) 20 W

(c) 40 W

(d) <u>60 W</u>

111. A thermistor has

(a) positive temperature coefficient

(b) negative temperature coefficient

(c) <u>zero temperature coefficient</u>

(d) variable temperature coefficient

112. If/, R and t are the current, resistance and time respectively, then according

to Joule's law heat produced will be proportional to

(a) <u>I2Rt</u>

(b) I2Rf

(c) I2R2t

(d) I2R2t*

113. Nichrome wire is an alloy of

(a) lead and zinc

(b) chromium and vanadium

(c) <u>nickel and chromium</u>

(d) copper and silver

114. When a voltage of one volt is applied, a circuit allows one micro ampere current to flow through it. The conductance of the circuit is

(a) <u>1 n-mho</u>

(b) 106 mho

(c) 1 milli-mho

(d) none of the above

115. Which of the following can have negative temperature coefficient ?

(a) Compounds of silver

(6) Liquid metals

(c) Metallic alloys

(d) <u>Electrolytes</u>

116. Conductance : mho ::

(a) <u>resistance : ohm</u>

(b) capacitance : henry

(c) inductance : farad

(d) lumen : steradian

117. 1 angstrom is equal to

(a) 10-8 mm

(b) 10″6 cm

(c) <u>10″10 m</u>

(d) 10~14 m

118. One newton meter is same as

(a) one watt

(b) <u>one joule</u>

(c) five joules

(d) one joule second

1. An air gap is usually inserted in magnetic circuits to

(a) increase m.m.f.

(b) increase the flux

(c) <u>prevent saturation</u>

(d) none of the above

2. The relative permeability of a ferromagnetic material is

(a) less than one

(b) more than one

(c) more than 10

(d) <u>more than 100 or 1000</u>

3. The unit of magnetic flux is

(a) henry

(b) <u>weber</u>

(c) ampereturn/weber

(d) ampere/metre

4. Permeability in a magnetic circuit corresponds to______ in an electric circuit.

(a) resistance

(b) resistivity

(c) <u>conductivity</u>

(d) conductance

5. Point out the wrong statement.

Magnetic leakage is undesirable in electric machines because it

(a) <u>lowers their power efficiency</u>

(b) increases their cost of manufacture

(c) leads to their increased weight

(d) produces fringing

6. Relative permeability of vacuum is

(a) <u>1</u>

(b) 1 H/m

(c) 1/4JI

(d) 4n x 10-' H/m

7. Permanent magnets are normally made of

(a) <u>alnico alloys</u>

(b) aluminium

(c) cast iron

(d) wrought iron

8. Energy stored by a coil is doubled when its current is increased by percent.

(a) 25

(b) 50

(c) <u>41.4</u>

(d) 100

9. Those magnetic materials are best suited for making armature and transformer

cores which have____permeability and________hystersis loss.

(a) high, high

(b) low, high

(c) <u>high, low</u>

(d) low, low

10. The rate of rise of current through an inductive coil is maximum

(a) at 63.2% of its maximum steady value

(b) <u>at the start of the current flow</u>

(c) after one time constant

(d) near the final maximum value of current

11. When both the inductance and resistance of a coil are doubled the value of

(a) <u>time constant remains unchanged</u>

(b) initial rate of rise of current is doubled

(c) final steady current is doubled

(d) time constant is halved

12. The initial rate of rise of current through a coil of inductance 10 H when

suddenly connected to a D.C. supply of 200 V is________Vs

(a) 50

(b) <u>20</u>

(c) 0.05

(d) 500

13. A material for good magnetic memory should have

(a) low hysteresis loss

(b) high permeability

(c) low retentivity

(d) <u>high retentivity</u>

14. Conductivity is analogous to

(a) retentivity

(b) resistivity

(c) <u>permeability</u>

(d) inductance

15. In a magnetic material hysteresis loss takes place primarily due to

(a) rapid reversals of its magnetisation

(b) flux density lagging behind magnetising force

(c) molecular friction

(d) <u>it high retentivity</u>

16. Those materials are well suited for making permanent magnets which have

______ retentivity and ________ coercivity.

(a) low, high

(b) <u>high, high</u>

(c) high, low

(d) low, low

17. If the area of hysteresis loop of a material is large, the hysteresis loss in this

material will be

(a) zero

(b) small

(c) <u>large</u>

(d) none of the above

18. Hard steel is suitable for making permanent magnets because

(a) <u>it has good residual magnetism</u>

(b) its hysteresis loop has large area

(c) its mechanical strength is high

(d) its mechanical strength is low

19. Silicon steel is used in electrical machines because it has

(a) low coercivity

(b) low retentivity

(c) <u>low hysteresis loss</u>

(d) high coercivity

20. Conductance is analogous to

(a) <u>permeance</u>

(b) reluctance

(c) flux

(d) inductance

21. The property of a material which opposes the creation of magnetic flux in it is

known as

(a) reluctivity

(b) magnetomotive force

(c) permeance

(d) <u>reluctance</u>

22. The unit of retentivity is

(a) weber

(b) <u>weber/sq. m</u>

(c) ampere turn/meter

(d) ampere turn

23. Reciprocal of reluctance is

(a) reluctivity

(b) <u>permeance</u>

(c) permeability

(d) susceptibility

24. While comparing magnetic and electric circuits, the flux of magnetic circuit is

compared with which parameter of electrical circuit ?

(a) E.m.f.

(b) <u>Current</u>

(c) Current density

(d) Conductivity

25. The unit of reluctance is

(a) metre/henry

(b) henry/metre

(c) henry

(d) <u>1/henry</u>

26. A ferrite core has less eddy current loss than an iron core because

(a) <u>ferrites have high resistance</u>

(b) ferrites are magnetic

(c) ferrites have low permeability

(d) ferrites have high hysteresis

27. Hysteresis loss least depends on

(a) volume of material

(b) frequency

(c) steinmetz coefficient of material

(d) <u>ambient temperature</u>

28. Laminated cores, in electrical machines, are used to reduce

(a) copper loss

(b) <u>eddy current loss</u>

(c) hysteresis loss

(d) all of the above

1. Tesla is a unit of

(a) field strength

(b) inductance

(c) <u>flux density</u>

(d) flux

2. A permeable substance is one

(a) which is a good conductor

(6) which is a bad conductor

(c) which is a strong magnet

(d) <u>through which the magnetic lines of force can pass very easily</u>

3. The materials having low retentivity are suitable for making

(a) weak magnets

(b) <u>temporary magnets</u>

(c) permanent magnets

(d) none of the above

4. A magnetic field exists around

(a) iron

(b) copper

(c) aluminium

(d) <u>moving charges</u>

5. Ferrites are materials.

(a) paramagnetic

(b) diamagnetic

(c) <u>ferromagnetic</u>

(d) none of the above

6. Air gap has_______eluctance as compared to iron or steel path
(a) little
(b) lower
(c) higher
(d) zero
7. The direction of magnetic lines of force is
(a) from south pole to north pole
(b) from north pole to south pole
(c) from one end of the magnet to another
(d) none of the above
8. Which of the following is a vector quantity ?
(a) Relative permeability
(b) Magnetic field intensity
(c) Flux density
(d) Magnetic potential
9. The two conductors of a transmission line carry equal current I in opposite
directions. The force on each conductor is
(a) proportional to 7
(b) proportional to X
(c) proportional to distance between the conductors
(d) inversely proportional to I
10. A material which is slightly repelled by a magnetic field is known as
(a) ferromagnetic material
(b) diamagnetic material
(c) paramagnetic material
(d) conducting material
11. When an iron piece is placed in a magnetic field
(a) the magnetic lines of force will bend away from their usual paths in order to go
away from the piece
(b) the magnetic lines of force will bend away from their usual paths in order to
pass through the piece
(c) the magnetic field will not be affected
(d) the iron piece will break
12. Fleming's left hand rule is used to find
(a) direction of magnetic field due to current carrying conductor

(b) direction of flux in a solenoid

(c) <u>direction of force on a current carrying conductor in a magnetic field</u>

(d) polarity of a magnetic pole

13. The ratio of intensity of magnetisation to the magnetisation force is known as

(a) flux density

(b) <u>susceptibility</u>

(c) relative permeability

(d) none of the above

14. Magnetising steel is normals difficult because

(a) it corrodes easily

(6) it has high permeability

(c) it has high specific gravity

(d) <u>it has low permeability</u>

15. The left hand rule correlates to

(a) current, induced e.m.f. and direction of force on a conductor

(b) magnetic field, electric field and direction of force on a conductor

(c) self induction, mutual induction and direction of force on a conductor

(d) <u>current, magnetic field and direction of force on a conductor</u>

16. The unit of relative permeability is

(a) henry/metre

(b) henry

(c) henry/sq. m

(d) <u>it is dimensionless</u>

17. A conductor of length L has current I passing through it, when it is placed

parallel to a magnetic field. The force experienced by the conductor will be

(a) <u>zero</u>

(b) BLI

(c) B2LI

(d) BLI2

18. The force between two long parallel conductors is inversely proportional to

(a) radius of conductors

(b) current in one conductor

(c) product of current in two conductors

(d) <u>distance between the conductors</u>

19. Materials subjected to rapid reversal of magnetism should have

(a) large area oiB-H loop

(b) <u>high permeability and low hysteresis loss</u>

(c) high co-ercivity and high retentivity

(d) high co-ercivity and low density

20. Indicate which of the following material does not retain magnetism permanently.

(a) <u>Soft iron</u>

(b) Stainless steel

(e) Hardened steel

(d) None of the above

21. The main constituent of permalloy is

(a) cobalt

(b) chromium

(c) <u>nickel</u>

(d) tungsten

22. The use of permanent magnets is. not made in

(a) magnetoes

(6) energy meters

(c) <u>transformers</u>

(d) loud-speakers

23. Paramagnetic materials have relative permeability

(a) slightly less than unity

(b) equal to unity

(c) <u>slightly more than unity</u>

(d) equal to that ferromagnetic mate rials

25. Substances which have permeability less than the permeability of free space

are known as

(a) ferromagnetic

(b) paramagnetic

(c) <u>diamagnetic</u>

(d) bipolar

27. In the left hand rule, forefinger always represents

(a) voltage

(b) current

(c) <u>magnetic field</u>

(d) direction of force on the conductor

28. Which of the following is a ferromagnetic material ?

(a) Tungsten

(b) Aluminium

(c) Copper

(d) <u>Nickel</u>

29. Ferrites are a sub-group of

(a) non-magnetic materials

(6) ferro-magnetic materials

(c) paramagnetic materials

(d) <u>ferri-magnetic materials</u>

30. Gilbert is a unit of

(a) electromotive force

(b) <u>magnetomotive force</u>

(c) conductance

(d) permittivity

51. Unit for quantity of electricity is

(a) ampere-hour

(b) watt

(c) joule

(d) <u>coulomb</u>

52. The Biot-savart's law is a general modification of

(a) Kirchhoffs law

(b) Lenz's law

(c) <u>Ampere's law</u>

(d) Faraday's laws

53. The most effective and quickest may of making a magnet from soft iron is by

(a) <u>placing it inside a coil carrying current</u>

(b) induction

(c) the use of permanent magnet

(d) rubbing with another magnet

54. The commonly used material for shielding or screening magnetism is

(a) copper

(b) aluminium

(c) <u>soft iron</u>

(d) brass

55. If a copper disc is rotated rapidly below a freely suspended magnetic needle,
the magnetic needle shall start rotating with a velocity
(a) less than that of disc but in opposite direction
(b) equal to that of disc and in the same direction
(c) equal to that of disc and in the opposite direction
(d) less than that of disc and in the same direction

56. A permanent magnet
(a) attracts some substances and repels others
(b) attracts all paramagnetic substances and repels others
(c) attracts only ferromagnetic substances
(d) attracts ferromagnetic substances and repels all others

57. The retentivity (a property) of material is useful for the construction of
(a) permanent magnets
(b) transformers
(c) non-magnetic substances
(d) electromagnets

58. The relative permeability of materials is not constant.
(a) diamagnetic
(b) paramagnetic
(c) ferromagnetic
(d) insulating

59. The materials are a bit inferior conductors of magnetic flux than air.
(a) ferromagnetic
(b) paramagnetic
(c) diamagnetic
(d) dielectric

60. Hysteresis loop in case of magnetically hard materials is more in shape as
compared to magnetically soft materials.
(a) circular
(b) triangular
(c) rectangular
(d) none of the above

61. A rectangular magnet of magnetic moment M is cut into two piece of same
length, the magnetic moment of each piece will be

(a) M

(b) <u>M/2</u>

(c) 2 M

(d) M/4

62. A keeper is used to

(a) change the direction of magnetic lines

(b) amplify flux

(c) restore lost flux

(d) <u>provide a closed path for flux</u>

63. Magnetic moment is a

(a) pole strength

(6) universal constant

(c) scalar quantity

(d) <u>vector quantity</u>

64. The change of cross-sectional area of conductor in magnetic field will affect

(a) reluctance of conductor

(b) resistance of conductor

(c) <u>(a) and (b) both in the same way</u>

(d) none of the above

65. The uniform magnetic field is

(a) the field of a set of parallel conductors

(b) the field of a single conductor

(c) <u>the field in which all lines of magnetic flux are parallel and equidistant</u>

(d) none of the above

66. The magneto-motive force is

(a) the voltage across the two ends of exciting coil

(b) the flow of an electric current

(c) <u>the sum of all currents embraced by one line of magnetic field</u>

(d) the passage of magnetic field through an exciting coil

91. For which of the following materials the saturation value is the highest ?

(a) Ferromagnetic materials

(6) Paramagnetic materials

(c) Diamagnetic materials

(d) <u>Ferrites</u>

92. The magnetic materials exhibit the property of magnetisation because of

(a) orbital motion of electrons

(b) spin of electrons

(c) spin of nucleus

(d) either of these

93. For which of the following materials the net magnetic moment should be zero ?

(a) Diamagnetic materials

(b) Ferrimagnetic materials

(c) Antiferromagnetic materials

(d) Antiferrimagnetic materials

94. The attraction capacity of electromagnet will increase if the

(a) core length increases i

(b) core area increases

(c) flux density decreases

(d) flux density increases

95. Which of the following statements is correct ?

(a) The conductivity of ferrites is better than ferromagnetic materials

(b) The conductivity of ferromagnetic materials is better than ferrites

(c) The conductivity of ferrites is very high

(d) The conductivity of ferrites is same as that of ferromagnetic materials

96. Temporary magnets are used in

(a) loud-speakers

(b) generators

(c) motors

(d) all of the above

97. Main causes of noisy solenoid are

(a) strong tendency of fan out of laminations at the end caused by repulsion

among magnetic lines of force

(b) uneven bearing surface, caused by dirt or uneven wear between moving and

stationary parts

(c) both of above

(d) none of the above

99. Core of an electromagnet should have

(a) low coercivity

(6) high susceptibility

(c) <u>both of the above</u>

(d) none of the above

100. Magnetism of a magnet can be destroyed by

(a) heating

(b) hammering

(c) by inductive action of another magnet

(d) <u>by all above methods</u>

1. The property of coil by which a counter e.m.f. is induced in it when the current

through the coil changes is known as

(a) <u>self-inductance</u>

(b) mutual inductance

(c) series aiding inductance

(d) capacitance

2. As per Faraday's laws of electromagnetic induction, an e.m.f. is induced in a

conductor whenever it

(a) lies perpendicular to the magnetic flux

(b) lies in a magnetic field

(c) <u>cuts magnetic flux</u>

(d) moves parallel to the direction of the magnetic field

3. Which of the following circuit element stores energy in the electromagnetic

field ?

(a) <u>Inductance</u>

(b) Condenser

(c) Variable resistor

(d) Resistance

4. The inductance of a coil will increase under all the following conditions except

(a) <u>when more length for the same number of turns is provided</u>

(6) when the number of turns of the coil increase

(c) when more area for each turn is provided

(d) when permeability of the core increases

5. Higher the self-inductance of a coil,

(a) lesser its weber-turns

(b) lower the e.m.f. induced

(c) greater the flux produced by it

(d) <u>longer the delay in establishing steady current through it</u>

6. In an iron cored coil the iron core is removed so that the coil becomes an air cored coil. The inductance of the coil will

(a) increase

(b) <u>decrease</u>

(c) remain the same

(d) initially increase and then decrease

7. An open coil has

(a) zero resistance and inductance

(b) <u>infinite resistance and zero inductance</u>

(c) infinite resistance and normal inductance

(d) zero resistance and high inductance

8. Both the number of turns and the core length of an inductive coil are doubled.

Its self-inductance will be

(a) unaffected

(b) <u>doubled</u>

(c) halved

(d) quadrupled

9. If current in a conductor increases then according to Lenz's law self-induced

voltage will

(a) aid the increasing current

(b) tend to decrease the amount of cur-rent

(c) <u>produce current opposite to the in-creasing current</u>

(d) aid the applied voltage

10. The direction of induced e.m.f. can be found by

(a) Laplace's law

(b) <u>Lenz's law</u>

(c) Fleming's right hand rule

(d) Kirchhoff s voltage law

11. Air-core coils are practically free from

(a) hysteresis losses

(b) eddy current losses

(c) <u>both (a) and (b)</u>

(d) none of the above

12. The magnitude of the induced e.m.f. in a conductor depends on the

(a) flux density of the magnetic field

(b) amount of flux cut

(c) amount of flux linkages

(d) rate of change of flux-linkages

13. Mutually inductance between two magnetically-coupled coils depends on

(a) permeability of the core

(b) the number of their turns

(c) cross-sectional area of their common core

(d) all of the above

14. A laminated iron core has reduced eddy-current losses because

(a) more wire can be used with less D.C. resistance in coil

(b) the laminations are insulated from each other

(c) the magnetic flux is concentrated in the air gap of the core

(d) the laminations are stacked vertfcally

15. The law that the induced e.m.f. and current always oppose the cause producing them is due to

(a) Faraday

(b) Lenz

(c) Newton

16. Which of the following is not a unit of inductance ?

(a) Henry

(b) Coulomb/volt ampere

(c) Volt second per ampere

(d) All of the above

17. In case of an inductance, current is proportional to

(a) voltage across the inductance

(b) magnetic field

(c) both (a) and (b)

(d) neither (a) nor (b)

18. Which of the following circuit elements will oppose the change in circuit

current ?

(a) Capacitance

(b) Inductance

(c) Resistance

(d) All of the above

19. For a purely inductive circuit which of the following is true ?

(a) Apparent power is zero

(b) Relative power is.zero

(c) Actual power of the circuit is zero

(d) Any capacitance even if present in the circuit will not be charged

20. Which of the following is unit of inductance ?

(a) Ohm

(b) Henry

(c) Ampere turns

(d) Webers/metre

21. An e.m.f. of 16 volts is induced in a coil of inductance 4H. The rate of change

of current must be

(a) 64 A/s

(b) 32 A/s

(c) 16 A/s

(d) 4 A/s

22. The core of a coil has a length of 200 mm. The inductance of coil is 6 mH. If

the core length is doubled, all other quantities, remaining the same, the inductance will be

(a) 3 mH

(b) 12 mH

(c) 24mH

(d)48mH

23. The self inductances of two coils are 8 mH and 18 mH. If the co-efficients of

coupling is 0.5, the mutual inductance of the coils is

(a) 4 mH

(b) 5 mH

(c) 6 mH

(d) 12 mH

24. Two coils have inductances of 8 mH and 18 mH and a co-efficient of coupling

of 0.5. If the two coils are connected in series aiding, the total inductance will be

(a) 32 mH

(b) 38 mH

(c) 40 mH

(d) 48 mH

25. A 200 turn coil has an inductance of 12 mH. If the number of turns is

increased to 400 turns, all other quantities (area, length etc.) remaining the same,

the inductance will be

(a) 6 mH

(b) 14 mH

(c) 24 mH

(d) 48 mH

26. Two coils have self-inductances of 10 H and 2 H, the mutual inductance being

zero. If the two coils are connected in series, the total inductance will be

(a) 6 H

(b) 8 H

(c) 12 H

(d) 24 H

27. In case all the flux from the current in coil 1 links with coil 2, the co-efficient

of coupling will be

(a) 2.0

(b) 1.0

(c) 0.5

(d) zero

28. A coil with negligible resistance has 50V across it with 10 mA. The inductive

reactance is

(a) 50 ohms

(b) 500 ohms

(c) 1000 ohms

(d) 5000 ohms

29. A conductor 2 meters long moves at right angles to a magnetic field of flux

density 1 tesla with a velocity of 12.5 m/s. The induced e.m.f. in the conductor will

be

(a) 10 V

(6) 15 V

(c) <u>25V</u>

(d) 50V

30. Lenz's law is a consequence of the law of conservation of

(a) induced current

(b) charge

(c) <u>energy</u>

(d) induced e.m.f.

31. A conductor carries 125 amperes of current under $60°$ to a magnetic field of 1.1

tesla. The force on the conductor will be

nearly

(a) 50 N

(b) <u>120 N</u>

(c) 240 N

(d) 480 N

32. Find the force acting on a conductor 3m long carrying a current of 50 amperes

at right angles to a magnetic field having a flux density of 0.67 tesla.

(a) <u>100 N</u>

(b) 400 N

(c) 600 N

(d) 1000 N

33. The co-efficient of coupling between two air core coils depends on

(a) self-inductance of two coils only

(b) mutual inductance between two coils only

(c) <u>mutual inductance and self inductance of two coils</u>

(d) none of the above

34. An average voltage of 10 V is induced in a 250 turns solenoid as a result of a

change in flux which occurs in 0.5 second. The total flux change is

(a) 20 Wb

(b) 2 Wb

(c) 0.2 Wb

(d) <u>0.02 Wb</u>

35. A 500 turns solenoid develops an average induced voltage of 60 V. Over what

time interval must a flux change of 0.06 Wb occur to produce such a voltage ?

(a) 0.01 s

(b) 0.1 s

(c) <u>0.5 s</u>

(d) 5 s

36. Which of the fpllowing inductor will have the least eddy current losses ?

(a) <u>Air core</u>

(b) Laminated iron core

(c) Iron core

(d) Powdered iron core

37. A coil induces 350 mV when the current changes at the rate of 1 A/ s. The

value of inductance is

(a) 3500 mH

(b) <u>350 mH</u>

(c) 250 mH

(d) 150 mH

38. Two 300 uH coils in series without mutual coupling have a total inductance of

(a) 300 uH

(b) <u>600 uH</u>

(c) 150 uH

(d) 75 uH

39. Current changing from 8 A to 12 A in one second induced 20 volts in a coil.

The value of inductance is

(a) 5 mH

(b) 10 mH

(c) <u>5 H</u>

(d) 10 H

40. Which circuit element(s) will oppose the change in circuit current ?

(a) Resistance only

(b) <u>Inductance only</u>

(c) Capacitance only

(d) Inductance and capacitance

41. A crack in the magnetic path of an inductor will result in

(a) unchanged inductance

(b) increased inductance

(c) zero inductance

(d) <u>reduced inductance</u>

42. A coil is wound on iron core which carries current I. The self-induced voltage
in the coil is not affected by

(a) variation in coil current

(b) <u>variation in voltage to the coil</u>

(c) change of number of turns of coil

(d) the resistance of magnetic path

1. Laminations of core are generally made of

(a) case iron

(b) carbon

(c) <u>silicon steel</u>

(d) stainless steel

2. Which of the following could be lamina-proximately the thickness of laminations of a D.C. machine ?

(a) 0.005 mm

(b) 0.05 mm

(c) <u>0.5 m</u>

(d) 5 m

3. The armature of D.C. generator is laminated to

(a) reduce the bulk

(b) provide the bulk

(c) insulate the core

(d) <u>reduce eddy current loss</u>

4. The resistance of armature winding depends on

(a) length of conductor

(b) cross-sectional area of the conductor

(c) number of conductors

(d) <u>all of the above</u>

5. The field coils of D.C. generator are usually made of

(a) mica

(b) <u>copper</u>

(c) cast iron

(d) carbon

6. The commutator segments are connected to the armature conductors by means of

(a) copper lugs

(b) resistance wires

(c) insulation pads

(d) brazing

7. In a commutator

(a) copper is harder than mica

(b) mica and copper are equally hard

(c) mica is harder than copper

(d) none of the above

8. In D.C. generators the pole shoes are fastened to the pole core by

(a) rivets

(b) counter sunk screws

(c) brazing

(d) welding

9. According to Fleming's right-hand rule for finding the direction of induced e.m.f., when middle finger points in the direction of induced e.m.f., forefinger will point in the direction of

(a) motion of conductor

(b) lines of force

(c) either of the above

(d) none of the above

10. Fleming's right-hand rule regarding direction of induced e.m.f., correlates

(a) magnetic flux, direction of current flow and resultant force

(b) magnetic flux, direction of motion and the direction of e.m.f. induced

(c) magnetic field strength, induced voltage and current

(d) magnetic flux, direction of force and direction of motion of conductor

11. While applying Fleming's right-hand rule to And the direction of induced e.m.f., the thumb points towards

(a) direction of induced e.m.f.

(b) direction of flux

(c) direction of motion of the conductor if forefinger points in the direction of generated e.m.f.

(d) <u>direction of motion of conductor, if forefinger points along the lines of flux</u>

12. The bearings used to support the rotor shafts are generally

(a) <u>ball bearings</u>

(b) bush bearings

(c) magnetic bearmgs

(d) needle bearings

13. In D.C. generators, the cause of rapid brush wear may be

(a) severe sparking

(b) rough commutator surface

(c) imperfect contact

(d) <u>any of the above</u>

14. In lap winding, the number of brushes is always

(a) double the number of poles

(b) <u>same as the number of poles</u>

(c) half the number of poles

(d) two

15. For a D.C. generator when the number of poles and the number of armature conductors is fixed, then which winding will give the higher e.m.f. ?

(a) Lap winding

(b) <u>Wave winding</u>

(c) Either of (a) and (b) above

(d) Depends on other features of design

16. In a four-pole D.C. machine

(a) all the four poles are north poles

(b) <u>alternate poles are north and south</u>

(c) all the four poles are south poles

(d) two north poles follow two south poles

17. Copper brushes in D.C. machine are used

(a) <u>where low voltage and high currents are involved</u>

(b) where high voltage and small cur-rents are involved

(c) in both of the above cases

(d) in none of the above cases

18. A separately excited generator as compared to a self-excited generator

(a) is amenable to better voltage control

(b) is more stable

(c) has exciting current independent of load current

(d) <u>has all above features</u>

19. In case of D.C. machines, mechanical losses are primary function of

(a) current

(b) voltage

(c) <u>speed</u>

(d) none of above

20. Iron losses in a D.C. machine are independent of variations in

(a) speed

(b) <u>load</u>

(c) voltage

(d) speed and voltage

21. In D.C. generators, current to the external circuit from armature is given through

(a) <u>commutator</u>

(b) solid connection

(c) slip rings

(d) none of above

23. Brushes of D.C. machines are made of

(a) <u>carbon</u>

(b) soft copper

(c) hard copper

(d) all of above

24. If B is the flux density, I the length of conductor and v the velocity of conductor, then induced e.m.f. is given by

(a)<u>Blv</u>

(b)Blv2

(c)Bl2v

(d)Bl2v2

25. In case of a 4-pole D.C. generator provided with a two layer lap winding with sixteen coils, the pole pitch will be

(a) 4

(b) <u>8</u>

(c) 16

(d) 32

26. The material for commutator brushes is generally

(a) mica

(b) copper

(c) cast iron

(d) <u>carbon</u>

27. The insulating material used between the commutator segments is normally

(a) graphite

(b) paper

(c) <u>mica</u>

(d) insulating varnish

28. In D.C. generators, the brushes on commutator remain in contact with conductors which

(a) lie under south pole

(b) lie under north pole

(c) <u>lie under interpolar region</u>

(d) are farthest from the poles

29. If brushes of a D.C. generator are moved in order to bring these brushes in

magnetic neutral axis, there will be

(a) demagnetisation only

(b) cross magnetisation as well as mag¬netisation

(c) <u>crossmagnetisation as well as demagnetising</u>

(d) cross magnetisation only

30. Armature reaction of an unsaturated D.C. machine is

(a) <u>crossmagnetising</u>

(b) demagnetising

(c) magnetising

(d) none of above

31. D.C. generators are connected to the busbars or disconnected from them only under the floating condition

(a) to avoid sudden loading of the primemover

(b) to avoid mechanicaljerk to the shaft

(c) to avoid burning of switch contacts

(d) <u>all above</u>

32. Eddy currents are induced in the pole shoes of a D.C. machine due to

(a) oscillating magnetic field

(b) pulsating magnetic flux

(c) <u>relative rotation between field and armature</u>

(d) all above

34. Equilizer rings are required in case armature is

(a) wave wound

(b) lap wound

(c) delta wound

(d) duplex wound

35. Welding generator will have

(a) lap winding

(b) wave winding

(c) delta winding

(d) duplex wave winding

36. In case of D.C. machine winding, number of commutator segments is equal to

(a) number of armature coils

(b) number of armature coil sides

(c) number of armature conductors

(d) number of armature turns

37. For a D.C. machines laboratory following type of D.C. supply will be suitable

(a) rotary converter

(b) mercury are rectifier

(c) induction motor D.C. generator set

(d) synchronous motor D.C. generator set

38. The function of pole shoes in the case of D.C. machine is

(a) to reduce the reluctance of the mag¬netic path

(b) to spread out the flux to achieve uniform flux density

(c) to support the field coil

(d) to discharge all the above functions

Ans: d

39. In the case of lap winding resultant pitch is

(a) multiplication of front and back pitches

(b) division of front pitch by back pitch

(c) sum of front and back pitches

(d) difference of front and back pitches

40. A D.C. welding generator has

(a) lap winding

(b) wave moving

(c) duplex winding

(d) any of the above

41. Which of the following statement about D.C. generators is false ?

(a) Compensating winding in a D.C. machine helps in commutation

(b) In a D. C. generator interpoles winding is connected in series with the armature winding

(c) Back pitch and front pitch are both odd and approximately equal to the pole pitch

(d) Equilizing bus bars are used with parallel running of D.C. shunt generators

42. The demagnetising component of armature reaction in a D.C. generator

(a) reduces generator e.m.f.

(b) increases armature speed

(c) reduces interpoles flux density

(d) results in sparking trouble

43. Magnetic field in a D.C. generator is produced by

(a) electromagnets

(b) permanent magnets

(c) both (a) and (b)

(d) none of the above

44. The number of brushes in a commutator depends on

(a) speed of armature

(b) type of winding

(c) voltage

(d) amount of current to be collected

45. Compensating windings are used in D.C. generators

(a) mainly to reduce the eddy currents by providing local short-circuits

(b) to provide path for the circulation of cooling air

(c) to neutralise the cross-magnetising effect of the armature reaction

(d) none of the above

46. Which of the following components of a D.C, generator plays vital role for

providing direct current of a D.C. generator ?

(a) Dummy coils

(b) Commutator

(c) Eye bolt

(d) Equilizer rings

47. In a D.C. generator the ripples in the direct e.m.f. generated are reduced by

(a) using conductor of annealed copper

(b) using commutator with large number of segments

(c) using carbon brushes of superior quality

(d) using equiliser rings

48. In D.C. generators, lap winding is used for

(a) high voltage, high current

(b) low voltage, high current

(c) high voltage, low current

(d) low voltage, low current

49. Two generators A and B have 6-poles each. Generator A has wave wound armature while generator B has lap wound armature. The ratio of the induced e.m.f. is generator A and B will be

(a) 2 : 3

(b) 3 : 1

(c) 3 : 2

(d) 1 : 3

50. The voltage drop for which of the following types of brush can be expected to be least ?

(a) Graphite brushes

(b) Carbon brushes

(c) Metal graphite brushes

(d) None of the above

51. The e.m.f. generated by a shunt wound D.C. generator isE. Now while pole flux remains constant, if the speed of the generator is doubled, the e.m.f. generated will be

(a) E/2

(b) 2E

(c) slightly less than E

(d) E

53. The armature core of a D.C. generator is usually made of

(a) silicon steel

(b) copper

(c) non-ferrous material

(d) cast-iron

54. Satisfactory commutation of D.C. machines requires

(a) brushes should be of proper grade and size

(b) brushes should smoothly run in the holders

(c) smooth, concentric commutator properly undercut

(d) all of the above

54a. Open circuited armature coil of a D.C. machine is

(a) identified by the scarring of the commutator segment to which open circuited coil is connected

(b) indicated by a spark completely around the commutator

(c) both (a) and (b)

(d) none of the above

56. For the parallel operation of two or more D.C. compound generators, we

should ensure that

(a) voltage of the incoming generator should be same as that of bus bar

(b) polarity of incoming generator should be same as that of bus bar

(c) all the series fields should be run in parallel by means of equilizer connection

(d) series fields of all generators should be either on positive side or negative side of the armature

57. D.C. series generator is used

(a) to supply traction load

(b) to supply industrial load at constant voltage

(c) voltage at the toad end of the feeder

(d) for none of the above purpose

58. Following D.C. generator will be in a position to build up without any residual magnetism in the poles

(a) series generator

(b) shunt generator

(c) compound generator

(d) self-excited generator

59. Interpole flux should be sufficient to

(a) neutralise the commutating self induced e.m.f.

(b) neutralise the armature reaction flux

(c) neutralise both the armature reaction flux as well as commutating e.m.f. induced in the coil

(d) perform none of the above functions

60. D.C. generator generally preferred for charging automobile batteries is

(a) series generator

(b) shunt generator

(c) long shunt compound generator

(d) any of'the above

61. In a D.C. generator the number of mechanical degrees and electrical degrees will be the same when

(a) r.p.m. is more than 300

(b) r.p.m. is less than 300

(c) number of poles is 4

(d) <u>number of poles is 2</u>

62. Permeance is the reciprocal of

(a) flux density

(b) <u>reluctance</u>

(c) ampere-turns

(d) resistance

63. In D.C. generators the polarity of the interpoles

(a) <u>is the same as that of the main pole ahead</u>

(b) is the same as that of the immediately preceding pole

(c) is opposite to that of the main pole ahead

(d) is neutral as these poles do not play part in generating e.m.f.

64. The e.m.f. generated in a D.C. generator is directly proportional to

(a) flux/pole

(b) <u>speed of armature</u>

(c) number of poles

(d) all of the above

65. In a D.C. generator the magnetic neutral axis coincides with the geometrical neutral axis, when

(a) <u>there is no load on the generator</u>

(b) the generator runs on full load

(c) the generator runs on overload

(d) the generator runs on designed speed

66. In a D.C. generator in order to reduce sparking at brushes, the self-induced e.m.f. in the coil is neutralised by all of the following except

(a) interpoles

(b) <u>dummy coils</u>

(c) compensating winding

(d) shifting of axis of brushes

67. In D.C. generators on no-load, the air gap flux distribution in space is

(a) sinusoidal

(b) triangular

(c) pulsating

(d) <u>flat topped</u>

68. A shunt generator running at 1000 r.p.m. has generated e.m.f. as 200 V. If the speed increases to 1200 r.p.m., the generated e.m.f. will be nearly

(a) 150 V

(b) 175 V

(c) 240 V

(d) 290 V

69. The purpose of providing dummy coils in a generator is

(a) to reduce eddy current losses

(b) to enhance flux density

(c) to amplify voltage

(d) to provide mechanical balance for the rotor

1. No-load speed of which of the following motor will be highest ?

(a) Shunt motor

(b) Series motor

(c) Cumulative compound motor

(d) Differentiate compound motor

2. The direction of rotation of a D.C. series motor can be changed by

(a) interchanging supply terminals

(b) interchanging field terminals

(c) either of (a) and (b) above

(d) None of the above

3. Which of the following application requires high starting torque ?

(a) Lathe machine

(b) Centrifugal pump

(c) Locomotive

(d) Air blower

4. If a D.C. motor is to be selected for conveyors, which rriotor would be preferred ?

(a) Series motor

(b) Shunt motor

(c) Differentially compound motor

(d) Cumulative compound motor

5. Which D.C. motor will be preferred for machine tools ?

(a) Series motor

(b) Shunt motor

(c) Cumulative compound motor

(d) Differential compound motor

6. Differentially compound D.C. motors can find applications requiring

(a) high starting torque

(b) <u>low starting torque</u>

(c) variable speed

(d) frequent on-off cycles

7. Which D.C. motor is preferred for elevators ?

(a) Shunt motor

(b) Series motor

(c) Differential compound motor

(d) <u>Cumulative compound motor</u>

8. According to Fleming's left-hand rule, when the forefinger points in the direction of the field or flux, the middle finger will point in the direction of

(a) <u>current in the conductor aovtaat of conductor</u>

(c) resultant force on conductor

(d) none of the above

9. If the field of a D.C. shunt motor gets opened while motor is running

(a) the speed of motor will be reduced %

(b) the armature current will reduce

(c) <u>the motor will attain dangerously high speed 1</u>

(d) the motor will continue to nuvat constant speed

10. Starters are used with D.C. motors because

(a) these motors have high starting torque

(b) these motors are not self-starting

(c) back e.m.f. of these motors is zero initially

(d) <u>to restrict armature current as there is no back e.m.f. while starting</u>

11. In D.C. shunt motors as load is reduced

(a) the speed will increase abruptly

(b) the speed will increase in proportion to reduction in load

(c) <u>the speed will remain almost/constant</u>

(d) the speed will reduce

12. A D.C. series motor is that which

(a) <u>has its field winding consisting of thick wire and less turns</u>

(b) has a poor torque

(c) can be started easily without load

(d) has almost constant speed

13. For starting a D.C. motor a starter is required because

(a) it limits the speed of the motor

(b) <u>it limits the starting current to a safe value</u>

(c) it starts the motor

(d) none of the above

14. The type of D.C. motor used for shears and punches is

(a) shunt motor

(b) series motor

(c) differential compoutid D.C. motor

(d) <u>cumulative compound D.C. motor</u>

15. If a D.C. motor is connected across the A.C. supply it will

(a) run at normal speed

(b) not run

(c) run at lower speed

(d) <u>burn due to heat produced in the field winding by .eddy currents</u>

16. To get the speed of D.C, motor below the normal without wastage of electrical energy is used.

(a) <u>Ward Leonard control</u>

(b) rheostatic control

(c) any of the above method

(d) none of the above method

17. When two D.C. series motors are connected in parallel, the resultant speed is

(a) more than the normal speed

(b) loss than the normal speed

(c) <u>normal speed</u>

(d) zero

18. The speed of a D.C. shunt motor more than its full-load speed can be obtained by

(a) <u>decreasing the field current</u>

(b) increasing the field current

(c) decreasing the armature current

(d) increasing the armature current

19. In a D.C. shunt motor, speed is

(a) <u>independent of armature current</u>

(b) directly proportional to the armature current

(c) proportional to the square of the current

(d) inversely proportional to the armature current

20. A direct on line starter is used: for starting motors

(a) <u>up to 5 H.P.</u>

(b) up to 10 H.P.

(c) up to 15 H.P.

(d) up to 20 H.P.

21. What will happen if the back e.m.f. of a D.C. motor vanishes suddenly?

(a) The motor will stop

(b) The motor will continue to run

(c) <u>The armature may burn</u>

(d) The motor will run noisy

22. In case of D.C. shunt motors the speed is dependent on back e.m.f. only because

(a) back e.m.f. is equal to armature drop

(b) armature drop is negligible

(c) flux is proportional to armature current

(d) <u>flux is practically constant in D:C. shunt motors</u>

23. In a D.C. shunt motor, under the conditions of maximum power, the current in the armature will be

(a) almost negligible

(b) rated full-load current

(c) less than full-load current

(d) <u>more than full-load current</u>

24. These days D.C. motors are widely used in

(a) pumping sets

(b) air compressors

(c) <u>electric traction</u>

(d) machine shops

25. By looking at which part of the motor, it can be easily confirmed that a particular motor is D.C. motor?

(a) Frame

(b) Shaft

(c) <u>Commutator</u>

(d) Stator

26. In which of the following applications D.C. series motor is invariably tried?

(a) <u>Starter for a car</u>

(b) Drive for a water pump

(c) Fan motor

(d) Motor operation in A.C. or D.C.

27. In D.C. machines fractional pitch winding is used

(a) to improve cooling

(b) to reduce copper losses

(c) to increase the generated e.m.f.

(d) <u>to reduce the sparking</u>

28. A three point starter is considered suitable for

(a) shunt motors

(b) <u>shunt as well as compound motors</u>

(c) shunt, compound and series motors

(d) all D.C. motors

29. In case-the conditions for maximum power for a D.C. motor are established, the efficiency of the motor will be

(a) 100%

(b) around 90%

(c) anywhere between 75% and 90%

(d) <u>less than 50%</u>

30. The ratio of starting torque to full-load torque is least in case of

(a) series motors

(b) <u>shunt motors</u>

(c) compound motors

(d) none of the above

31. In D.C. motor which of the following can sustain the maximum temperature rise?

(a) Slip rings

(b) Commutator

(c) <u>Field winding</u>

(d) Armature winding

33. Which of the following law/rule can he used to determine the direction of rotation of D.C. motor ?

(a) Lenz's law

(b) Faraday's law

(c) Coloumb's law

(d) <u>Fleming's left-hand rule</u>

34. Which of the following load normally needs starting torque more than the rated torque?

(a) Blowers

(b) <u>Conveyors</u>

(c) Air compressors

(d) Centrifugal pumps

35. The starting resistance of a D.C. motor is generally

(a) <u>low</u>

(b) around 500 Q

(c) 1000 Q

(d) infinitely large

36. The speed of a D.C. series motor is

(a) proportional to the armature current

(b) proportional to the square of the armature current

(c) proportional to field current

(d) <u>inversely proportional to the armature current</u>

37. In a D.C. series motor, if the armature current is reduced by 50%, the torque of the motor will be equal to

(a) 100% of the previous value

(b) 50% of the previous value

(c) <u>25% of the previous value</u>

(d) 10% of the previous value

38. The current drawn by the armature of D.C. motor is directly proportional to

(a) <u>the torque required</u>

(b) the speed of the motor

(c) the voltage across the terminals

(d) none of the above

39. The power mentioned on the name plate of an electric motor indicates

(a) the power drawn in kW

(b) the power drawn in kVA

(c) the gross power

(d) <u>the output power available at the shaft</u>

40. Which D.C. motor has got maximum self loading property?

(a) Series motor

(b) Shunt motor

(c) Cumulatively compounded 'motor

(d) <u>Differentially compounded motor</u>

41. Which D.C. motor will be suitable along with flywheel for intermittent light and heavy loads?

(a) Series motor

(b) Shunt motor

(c) <u>Cumulatively compounded motor</u>

(d) Differentially compounded motor

42. If a D.C. shunt motor is working at no load and if shunt field circuit suddenly opens

(a) nothing will happen to the motor

(b) this will make armature to take heavy current, possibly burning it

(c) <u>this will result in excessive speed, possibly destroying armature due to excessive centrifugal stresses</u>

(d) motor will run at very slow speed

43. D.C. series motors are used

(a) where load is constant

(b) where load changes frequently

(c) where constant operating speed is needed

(d) <u>in none of the above situations.</u>

44. For the same H.P. rating and full load speed, following motor has poor starting torque

(a) shunt

(b) series

(c) <u>differentially compounded</u>

(d) cumulativelyc'ompounded

45. In case of conductively compensated D.C. series motors, the compensating winding is provided

(a) as separately wound unit

(6) in parallel with armature winding

(c) <u>in series with armature winding</u>

(d) in parallel with field winding

46. Sparking at the commutator of a D.C. motor may result in

(a) damage to commutator segments

(b) damage to commutator insulation

(c) increased power consumption

(d) <u>all of the above</u>

47. Which of the following motor is preferred for operation in highly explosive atmosphere ?

(a) Series motor

(b) Shunt motor

(c) <u>Air motor</u>

(d) Battery operated motor

48. If the supply voltage for a D.C. motor is increased, which of the following will decrease ?

(a) Starting torque

(b) Operating speed

(c) Full-load current

(d) All of the above

49. Which one of the following is not the function of pole shoes in a D.C. machine ?

(a) To reduce eddy current loss

(b) To support the field coils

(c) To spread out flux for better uniformity

(d) To reduce the reluctance of the magnetic path

50. The mechanical power developed by a shunt motor will be maximum when the ratio of back e.m.f. to applied voltage is

(a) 4.0

(b) 2.0

(c) 1.0

(d) 0.5

51. The condition for maximum power in case of D.C. motor is

(a) back e.m.f. = 2 x supply voltage

(b) back e.m.f. = | x supply voltage

(c) supply voltage = | x back e.m.f.

(d) supply voltage = back e.m.f.

52. For which of the following applications a D.C. motor is preferred over an A.C. motor ?

(a) Low speed operation

(b) High speed operation

(c) Variable speed operation

(d) Fixed speed operation

53. In D.C. machines the residual magnetism is of the order of

(a) 2 to 3 per cent

(6) 10 to 15 per cent

(c) 20 to 25 per cent

(d) 50 to 75 per cent

54. Which D.C. motor is generally preferred for cranes and hoists ?

(a) Series motor

(b) Shunt motor

(c) Cumulatively compounded motor

(d) Differentially compounded motor

55. Three point starter can be used for

(a) series motor only

(b) shunt motor only

(c) compound motor only

(d) <u>both shunt and compound motor</u>

56. Sparking, is discouraged in a D.C. motor because

(a) it increases the input power con-sumption

(b) <u>commutator gets damaged</u>

(c) both (a) and (b)

(d) none of the above

57. Speed control by Ward Leonard method gives uniform speed variation

(a) in one direction

(b) <u>in both directions</u>

(c) below normal speed only

(d) above normal speed only.

58. Flywheel is used with D.C. compound motor to reduce the peak demand by the motor, compound motor will have to be

(a) level compounded

(b) under compounded

(c) <u>cumulatively compounded</u>

(d) differentially compounded

59. Following motor is used where high starting torque and wide speed range control is required.

(a) Single phase capacitor start

(b) Induction motor

(c) Synchronous motor

(d) <u>D.C. motor</u>

60. In a differentially compounded D.C. motor, if shunt field suddenly opens

(a) <u>the motor will first stop and then run in opposite direction as series motor</u>

(b) the motor will work as series motor and run at slow speed in the same direction

(c) the motor will work as series motor and run at high speed in the same direction

(d) the motor will not work and come to stop

61. Which of the following motor has the poorest speed regulation ?

(a) Shunt motor

(b) <u>Series motor</u>

(c) Differential compound motor

(d) Cumulative compound motor

62. Buses, trains, trolleys, hoists, cranes require high starting torque and therefore make use of

(a) <u>D.C. series motor</u>

(b) D.C. shunt motor

(c) induction motor

(d) all of above motors

63. As -the load is increased the speed of D.C. shunt motor will

(a) <u>reduce slightly</u>

(b) increase slightly

(c) increase proportionately

(d) remains unchanged

64. The armature torque of the D.C. shunt motor is proportional to

(a) field flux only

(b) <u>armature current only</u>

(c) both (a) and (b)

(d) none of the above

65. Which of the following method of speed control of D.C. machine will offer minimum efficiency ?

(a) Voltage control method

(b) Field control method

(c) <u>Armature control method</u>

(d) All above methods

1. Which of the following component is usually fabricated out of silicon steel ?

(a) Bearings

(b) Shaft

(c) <u>Statorcore</u>

(d) None of the above

2. The frame of an induction motor is usually made of

(a) silicon steel

(b) <u>cast iron</u>

(c) aluminium

(d) bronze

3. The shaft of an induction motor is made of

(a) <u>stiff</u>

(b) flexible

(c) hollow

(d) any of the above

4. The shaft of an induction motor is made of

(a) high speed steel

(b) stainless steel

(c) <u>carbon steel</u>

(d) cast iron

5. In an induction motor, no-load the slip is generally

(a) <u>less than 1%</u>

(b) 1.5%

(c) 2%

(d) 4%

6. In medium sized induction motors, the slip is generally around

(a) 0.04%

(b) 0.4%

(c) <u>4%</u>

(d) 14%

7. In squirrel cage induction motors, the rotor slots are usually given slight skew

in order to

(a) reduce windage losses

(b) reduce eddy currents

(c) reduce accumulation of dirt and dust

(d) <u>reduce magnetic hum</u>

8. In case the air gap in an induction motor is increased

(a) the magnetising current of the rotor will decrease

(b) <u>the power factor will decrease</u>

(c) speed of motor will increase

(d) the windage losses will increase

9. Slip rings are usually made of

(a) copper

(b) carbon

(c) <u>phospor bronze</u>

(d) aluminium

10. A 3-phase 440 V, 50 Hz induction motor has 4% slip. The frequency of rotor

e.m.f. will be

(a) 200 Hz

(b) 50 Hz

(c) 2 Hz

(d) 0.2 Hz

11. In Ns is the synchronous speed and s the slip, then actual running speed of an

induction motor will be

(a) Ns

(b) s.N,

(c) (1-s)Ns

(d) (Ns-1)s

The efficiency of an induction motor can be expected to be nearly

(a) 60 to 90%

(b) 80 to 90%

(c) 95 to 98%

(d) 99%

13. The number of slip rings on a squirrel cage induction motor is usually

(a) two

(b) three

(c) four

(d) none

14. The starting torque of a squirrel-cage induction motor is

(a) low

(b) negligible

(c) same as full-load torque

(d) slightly more than full-load torque

15. A double squirrel-cage induction motor has

(a) two rotors moving in oppsite direction

(b) two parallel windings in stator

(c) two parallel windings in rotor

(d) two series windings in stator

16. Star-delta starting of motors is not possible in case of

(a) single phase motors

(b) variable speed motors

(c) low horse power motors

(d) high speed motors

17. The term 'cogging' is associated with

(a) three phase transformers

(b) compound generators

(c) D.C. series motors

(d) <u>induction motors</u>

18. In case of the induction motors the torque is

(a) inversely proportional to (Vslip)

(b) directly proportional to (slip)2

(c) inversely proportional to slip

(d) <u>directly proportional to slip</u>

19. An induction motor with 1000 r.p.m. speed will have

(a) 8 poles

(b) <u>6 poles</u>

(c) 4 poles

(d) 2 poles

20. The good power factor of an induction motor can be achieved if the average

flux density in the air gap is

(a) absent

(b) <u>small</u>

(c) large

(d) infinity

21. An induction motor is identical to

(a) D.C. compound motor

(b) D.C. series motor

(c) synchronous motor

(d) <u>asynchronous motor</u>

22. The injected e.m.f. in the rotor of induction motor must have

(a) zero frequency

(b) <u>the same frequency as the slip frequency</u>

(c) the same phase as the rotor e.m.f.

(d) high value for the satisfactory speed control

23. Which of the following methods is easily applicable to control the speed of the

squirrel-cage induction motor ?

(a) <u>By changing the number of stator poles</u>

(b) Rotor rheostat control

(c) By operating two motors in cascade

(d) By injecting e.m.f. in the rotor circuit

24. The crawling in the induction motor is caused by

(a) low voltage supply

(b) high loads

(c) harmonics develped in the motor

(d) improper design of the machine

(e) none of the above

25. The auto-starters (using three auto transformers) can be used to start cage

induction motor of the following type

(a) star connected only

(b) delta connected only

(c) (a) and (b) both

(d) none of the above

26. The torque developed in the cage induction motor with autostarter is

(a) k/torque with direct switching

(6) K x torque with direct switching

(c) K2 x torque with direct switching

(d) k2/torque with direct switching

27. When the equivalent circuit diagram of doouble squirrel-cage induction motor

is constructed the two cages can be

considered

(a) in series

(b) in parallel

(c) in series-parallel

(d) in parallel with stator

28. It is advisable to avoid line-starting of induction motor and use starter

because

(a) motor takes five to seven times its full load current

(b) it will pick-up very high speed and may go out of step

(c) it will run in reverse direction

(d) starting torque is very high

29. Stepless speed control of induction motor is possible by which of the following methods ?

(a) e.m.f. injection in rotor eueuit

(b) Changing the number of poles

(c) Cascade operation

(d) None of the above

30. Rotor rheostat control method of speed control is used for
(a) squirrel-cage induction motors only
(b) slip ring induction motors only
(c) both (a) and (b)
(d) none of the above

31. In the circle diagram for induction motor, the diameter of the circle represents
(a) slip
(b) rotor current
(c) running torque
(d) line voltage

32. For which motor the speed can be controlled from rotor side ?
(a) Squirrel-cage induction motor
(b) Slip-ring induction motor
(c) Both (a) and (b)
(d) None of the above

33. If any two phases for an induction motor are interchanged
(a) the motor will run in reverse direction
(b) the motor will run at reduced speed
(c) the motor will not run
(d) the motor will burn

34. An induction motor is
(a) self-starting with zero torque
(b) self-starting with high torque
(c) self-starting with low torque
(d) non-self starting

35. The maximum torque in an induction motor depends on
(a) frequency
(b) rotor inductive reactance
(c) square of supply voltage
(d) all of the above

36. In three-phase squirrel-cage induction motors
(a) rotor conductor ends are short-circuited through slip rings
(b) rotor conductors are short-circuited through end rings
(c) rotor conductors are kept open
(d) rotor conductors are connected to insulation

37. In a three-phase induction motor, the number of poles in the rotor winding is always

(a) zero

(b) more than the number of poles in stator

(c) less than number of poles in stator

(d) <u>equal to number of poles in stator</u>

38. DOL starting of induction motors is usually restricted to

(a) <u>low horsepower motors</u>

(b) variable speed motors

(c) high horsepower motors

(d) high speed motors

39. The speed of a squirrel-cage induction motor can be controlled by all of the

following except

(a) changing supply frequency

(b) changing number of poles

(c) <u>changing winding resistance</u>

(d) reducing supply voltage

40. The 'crawling" in an induction motor is caused by

(a) high loads

(6) low voltage supply

(c) improper design of machine

(d) <u>harmonics developed in the motor</u>

41. The power factor of an induction motor under no-load conditions will be

closer to

(a) <u>0.2 lagging</u>

(b) 0.2 leading

(c) 0.5 leading

(d) unity

42. The 'cogging' of an induction motor can be avoided by

(a) proper ventilation

(b) using DOL starter

(c) auto-transformer starter

(d) <u>having number of rotor slots more or less than the number of stator slots (not equal)</u>

43. If an induction motor with certain ratio of rotor to stator slots, runs at 1/7 of the normal speed, the phenomenon will be termed as

(a) humming

(b) hunting

(c) <u>crawling</u>

(d) cogging

44. Slip of an induction motor is negative when

(a) magnetic field and rotor rotate in opposite direction

(b) rotor speed is less than the synchronous speed of the field and are in the same direction

(c) <u>rotor speed is more than the synchronous speed of the field and are in the same direction</u>

(d) none of the above

45. Size of a high speed motor as compared to low speed motor for the same H.P. will be

(a) bigger

(b) <u>smaller</u>

(c) same

(d) any of the above

46. A 3-phase induction motor stator delta connected, is carrying full load and one of its fuses blows out. Then the motor

(a) <u>will continue running burning its one phase</u>

(b) will continue running burning its two phases

(c) will stop and carry heavy current causing permanent damage to its winding

(d) will continue running without any harm to the winding

47. A 3-phase induction motor delta connected is carrying too heavy load and oneof its fuses blows out. Then the motor

(a) will continue running burning its one phase

(b) will continue running burning its two phase

(c) <u>will stop and carry heavy current causing permanent damage to its winding</u>

(d) will continue running without any harm to the winding

48. Low voltage at motor terminals is due to

(a) inadequate motor wiring

(b) poorely regulated power supply

(c) <u>any one of the above</u>

(d) none of the above

49. In an induction motor the relationship between stator slots and rotor slots is that

(a) stator slots are equal to rotor slots

(b) stator slots are exact multiple of rotor slots

(c) <u>stator slots are not exact multiple of rotor slots</u>

(d) none of the above

50. Slip ring motor is recommended where

(a) speed control is required

(6) frequent starting, stopping and reversing is required

(c) high starting torque is needed

(d) <u>all above features are required</u>

51. As load on an induction motor goes on increasing

(a) its power factor goes on decreasing

(b) its power factor remains constant

(c) its power factor goes on increasing even after full load

(d) <u>its power factor goes on increasing up to full load and then it falls again</u>

52. If a 3-phase supply is given to the stator and rotor is short circuited rotor will move

(a) in the opposite direction as the direction of the rotating field

(b) <u>in the same direction as the direction of the field</u>

(c) in any direction depending upon phase squence of supply

53. It is advisable to avoid line starting of induction motor and use starter because

(a) it will run in reverse direction

(b) it will pick up very high speed and may go out of step

(c) <u>motor takes five to seven times its full load current</u>

(d) starting torque is very high

54. The speed characteristics of an induction motor closely resemble the speedload characteristics of which of the following machines

(a) D.C. series motor

(b) <u>D.C. shunt motor</u>

(c) universal motor

(d) none of the above

55. Which type of bearing is provided in small induction motors to support the rotor shaft ?

(a) <u>Ball bearings</u>

(b) Cast iron bearings

(c) Bush bearings

(d) None of the above

56. A pump induction motor is switched on to a supply 30% lower than its rated voltage. The pump runs. What will eventually happen ? It will

(a) stall after sometime

(b) stall immediately

(c) continue to run at lower speed without damage

(d) get heated and subsequently get damaged

57. 5 H.P., 50-Hz, 3-phase, 440 V, induction motors are available for the following r.p.m. Which motor will be the costliest ?

(a) 730 r.p.m.

(b) 960 r.p.m.

(c) 1440 r.p.m.

(d) 2880 r.p.m.

58. A 3-phase slip ring motor has

(a) double cage rotor

(b) wound rotor

(c) short-circuited rotor

(d) any of the above

59. The starting torque of a 3-phase squirrel cage induction motor is

(a) twice the full load torque

(b) 1.5 times the full load torque

(c) equal to full load torque

60. Short-circuit test on an induction motor cannot be used to determine

(a) windage losses

(b) copper losses

(c) transformation ratio

(d) power scale of circle diagram

61. In a three-phase induction motor

(a) iron losses in stator will be negligible as compared to that in rotor

(6) iron losses in motor will be neg¬ligible as compared to that in rotor

(c) iron losses in stator will be less than that in rotor

(d) iron losses in stator will be more than that in rotor

62. In case of 3-phase induction motors, plugging means

(a) pulling the motor directly on line without a starter

(b) locking of rotor due to harmonics

(c) starting the motor on load which is more than the rated load

(d) interchanging two supply phases for quick stopping

63. Which is of the following data is required to draw the circle diagram for an induction motor ?

(a) Block rotor test only

(b) No load test only

(c) Block rotor test and no-load test

(d) <u>Block rotor test, no-load test and stator resistance test</u>

64. In three-phase induction motors sometimes copper bars are placed deep in the rotor to

(a) <u>improve starting torque</u>

(b) reduce copper losses

(c) improve efficiency

(d) improve power factor

65. In a three-phase induction motor

(a) power factor at starting is high as compared to that while running

(b) <u>power factor at starting is low as compared to that while running</u>

(c) power factor at starting in the same as that while running

66. The vafcie of transformation ratio of an induction motor can be found by

(a) open-circuit test only

(b) <u>short-circuit test only</u>

(c) stator resistance test

(d) none of the above

67. The power scale of circle diagram of an induction motor can be found from

(a) stator resistance test

(b) no-load test only

(c) <u>short-circuit test only</u>

(d) noue of the above

68. The shape of the torque/slip curve of induction motor is

(a) parabola

(b) hyperbola

(c) <u>rectangular parabola</u>

(d) straigth line

69. A change of 4% of supply voltage to an induction motor will produce a change of approximately

(a) 4% in the rotor torque

(b) 8% in the rotor torque

(c) 12% in the rotor torque

(d) <u>16% in the rotor torque</u>

70. The stating torque of the slip ring induction motor can be increased by adding

(a) external inductance to the rotor

(b) <u>external resistance to the rotor</u>

(c) external capacitance to the rotor

(d) both resistance and inductance to rotor

71. A 500 kW, 3-phase, 440 volts, 50 Hz, A.C. induction motor has a speed of 960 r.p.m. on full load. The machine has 6 poles. The slip of the machine will be

(a) 0.01

(b) 0.02

(c) 0.03

(d) <u>0.04</u>

72. The complete circle diagram of induetion motor can be drawn with the help of

data found from

(a) noload test

(6) blocked rotor test

(c) stator resistance test

(d) <u>all of the above</u>

73. In the squirrel-cage induction motor the rotor slots are usually given slight skew

(a) <u>to reduce the magnetic hum and locking tendency of the rotor</u>

(b) to increase the tensile strength of the rotor bars

(c) to ensure easy fabrication

(d) none of the above

74. The torque of a rotor in an induction motor under running condition is maximum

(a) at the unit value of slip

(b) at the zero value of slip

(c) <u>at the value of the slip which makes rotor reactance per phase equal to the resistance per phase</u>

(d) at the value of the slip which makes the rotor reactance half of the rotor

75. What will happen if the relative speed between the rotating flux of stator and rotor of the induction motor is zero ?

(a) The slip of the motor will be 5%

(b) <u>The rotor will not run</u>

(c) The rotor will run at very high speed

(d) The torque produced will be very large

76. The circle diagram for an induction motor cannot be used to determine

(a) <u>efficiency</u>

(b) power factor

(c) frequency

(d) output

77. Blocked rotor test on induction motors is used to find out

(a) leakage reactance

(b) power factor on short circuit

(c) short-circuit current under rated voltage

(d) <u>all of the above</u>

78. Lubricant used for ball bearing is usually

(a) graphite

(b) <u>grease</u>

(c) mineral oil

(d) molasses

79. An induction motor can run at synchronous speed when

(a) it is run on load

(b) it is run in reverse direction

(c) it is run on voltage higher than the rated voltage

(d) <u>e.m.f. is injected in the rotor circuit</u>

80. Which motor is preferred for use in mines where explosive gases exist ?

(a) <u>Air motor</u>

(b) Induction motor

(c) D.C. shunt motor

(d) Synchronous motor

81. The torque developed by a 3-phase induction motor least depends on

(a) rotor current

(b) rotor power factor

(c) rotor e.m.f.

(d) <u>shaft diameter</u>

82. In an induction motor if air-gap is increased

(a) <u>the power factor will be low</u>

(b) windage losses will be more

(c) bearing friction will reduce

(d) copper loss will reduce In an induction motor

83. In induction motor, percentage slip depends on

(a) supply frequency

(b) supply voltage

(c) <u>copper losses in motor</u>

(d) none of the above

85. In case of a double cage induction motor, the inner cage has

(a) <u>high inductance arid low resistance</u>

(b) low inductance and high resistance

(c) low inductance and low resistance

(d) high inductance and high resistance

86. The low power factor of induction motor is due to

(a) rotor leakage reactance

(b) stator reactance

(c) the reactive lagging magnetizing current necessary to generate the magnetic flux

(d) <u>all of the above</u>

87. Insertion of reactance in the rotor circuit

(a) <u>reduces starting torque as well as maximum torque</u>

(b) increases starting torque as well as maximum torque

(c) increases starting torque but maxi-mum torque remains unchanged

(d) increases starting torque but maxi-mum torque decreases

88. Insertion of resistance in the rotcir of an induction motor to develop a given torque

(a) decreases the rotor current

(b) increases the rotor current

(c) rotor current becomes zero

(d) <u>rotor current rernains same</u>

89. For driving high inertia loods best type of induction motor suggested is

(a) <u>slip ring type</u>

(b) squirrel cage type

(c) any of the above

(d) none of the above

90. Temperature of the stator winding of a three phase induction motor is

obtained by

(a) resistance rise method

(b) thermometer method

(c) embedded temperature method

(d) <u>all above methods</u>

91. The purpose of using short-circuit gear is

(a) <u>to short circuit the rotor at slip rings</u>

(b) to short circuit the starting resistances in the starter

(c) to short circuit the stator phase of motor to form star

(d) none of the above

92. In a squirrel cage motor the induced e.m.f. is

(a) dependent on the shaft loading

(b) dependent on the number of slots

(c) <u>slip times the stand still e.m.f. induced in the rotor</u>

(d) none of the above

93. Less maintenance troubles are experienced in case of

(a) slip ring induction motor

(b) <u>squirrel cage induction motor</u>

(c) both (a) and (b)

(d) none of the above

94. A squirrel cage induction motor is not selected when

(a) initial cost is the main consideration

(b) maintenance cost is to be kept low

(c) <u>higher starting torque is the main consideration</u>

(d) all above considerations are involved

95. Reduced voltage starter can be used with

(a) slip ring motor only but not with squirrel cage induction motor

(b) squirrel cage induction motor only but not with slip ring motor

(c) <u>squirrel cage as well as slip ring induction motor</u>

(d) none of the above

96. Slip ring motor is preferred over squirrel cage induction motor where

(a) <u>high starting torque is required</u>

(b) load torque is heavy

(c) heavy pull out torque is required

(d) all of the above

97. In a star-delta starter of an induction motor

(a) resistance is inserted in the stator

(b) reduced voltage is applied to the stator

(c) resistance is inserted in the rotor

(d) <u>applied voltage perl stator phase is 57.7% of the line voltage</u>

98. The torque of an induction motor is

(a) <u>directly proportional to slip</u>

(b) inversely proportional to slip

(c) proportional to the square of the slip

(d) none of the above

99. The rotor of an induction motor runs at

(a) synchronous speed

(b) below synchronous speed

(c) above synchronous speed

(d) any of the above

100. The starting torque of a three phase induction motor can be increased by

(a) increasing slip

(b) increasing current

(c) both (a) and (b)

(d) none of the above

1. Which of the following does not change in a transformer ?

(a) Current

(b) Voltage

(c) Frequency

(d) All of the above

2. In a transformer the energy is conveyed from primary to secondary

(a) through cooling coil

(b) through air

(c) by the flux

(d) none of the above

3. A transformer core is laminated to

(a) reduce hysteresis loss

(b) reduce eddy current losses

(c) reduce copper losses

(d) reduce all above losses

4. The degree of mechanical vibrations produced by the laminations of a transformer depends on

(a) tightness of clamping

(b) gauge of laminations

(c) size of laminations

(d) all of the above

5. The no-load current drawn by transformer is usually what per cent of the full load current ?

(a) 0.2 to 0.5 per cent

(b) <u>2 to 5 per cent</u>

(c) 12 to 15 per cent

(d) 20 to 30 per cent

6. The path of a magnetic flux in a transformer should have

(a) high resistance

(b) high reluctance

(c) low resistance

(d) <u>low reluctance</u>

7. No-load on a transformer is carried out to determine

(a) copper loss

(b) magnetising current

(c) <u>magnetising current and loss</u>

(d) efficiency of the transformer

8. The dielectric strength of transformer oil is expected to be

(a) lkV

(b) <u>33 kV</u>

(c) 100 kV

(d) 330 kV

9. Sumpner's test is conducted on trans-formers to determine

(a) <u>temperature</u>

(b) stray losses

(c) all-day efficiency

(d) none of the above

10. The permissible flux density in case of cold rolled grain oriented steel is around

(a) <u>1.7 Wb/m2</u>

(b) 2.7 Wb/m2

(c) 3.7 Wb/m2

(d) 4.7 Wb/m2

11. The efficiency of a transformer will be maximum when

(a) copper losses = hysteresis losses

(b) hysteresis losses = eddy current losses

(c) eddy current losses = copper losses

(d) <u>copper losses = iron losses</u>

12. No-load current in a transformer

(a) <u>lags behind the voltage by about 75°</u>

(b) leads the voltage by about 75°

(c) lags behind the voltage by about 15°

(d) leads the voltage by about 15°

13. The purpose of providing an iron core in a transformer is to

(a) provide support to windings

(b) reduce hysteresis loss

(c) <u>decrease the reluctance of the magnetic path</u>

(d) reduce eddy current losses

14. Which of the following is not a part of transformer installation ?

(a) Conservator

(b) Breather

(c) Buchholz relay

(d) <u>Exciter</u>

15. While conducting short-circuit test on a transformer the following side is short circuited

(a) High voltage side

(b) <u>Low voltage side</u>

(c) Primary side

(d) Secondary side

16. In the transformer following winding has got more cross-sectional area

(a) <u>Low voltage winding</u>

(b) High voltage winding

(c) Primary winding

(d) Secondary winding

17. A transformer transforms

(a) voltage

(b) current

(c) <u>power</u>

(d) frequency

18. A transformer cannot raise or lower the voltage of a D.C. supply because

(a) there is no need to change the D.C. voltage

(b) a D.C. circuit has more losses

(c) <u>Faraday's laws of electromagnetic induction are not valid since the rate of change of flux is zero</u>

(d) none of the above

19. Primary winding of a transformer

(a) is always a low voltage winding

(b) is always a high voltage winding

(c) could either be a low voltage or high voltage winding

(d) none of the above

20. Which winding in a transformer has more number of turns ?

(a) Low voltage winding

(b) High voltage winding

(c) Primary winding

(d) Secondary winding

21. Efficiency of a power transformer is of the order of

(a) 100 per cent

(b) 98 per cent

(c) 50 per cent

(d) 25 per cent

22. In a given transformer for given applied voltage, losses which remain constant irrespective of load changes are

(a) friction and windage losses

(b) copper losses

(c) hysteresis and eddy current losses

(d) none of the above

23. A common method of cooling a power transformer is

(a) natural air cooling

(b) air blast cooling

(c) oil cooling

(d) any of the above

24. The no load current in a transformer lags behind the applied voltage by an angle of about

(a) 180°

(b) 120″

(c) 90°

(d) 75°

25. In a transformer routine efficiency depends upon

(a) supply frequency

(b) load current

(c) power factor of load

(d) both (b) and (c)

26. In the transformer the function of a conservator is to

(a) provide fresh air for cooling the transformer

(b) supply cooling oil to transformer in time of need

(c) protect the transformer from damage when oil expends due to heating

(d) none of the above

27. Natural oil cooling is used for transformers up to a rating of

(a) 3000 kVA

(b) 1000 kVA

(c) 500 kVA

(d) 250 kVA

28. Power transformers are designed to have maximum efficiency at

(a) nearly full load

(b) 70% full load

(c) 50% full load

(d) no load

29. The maximum efficiency of a distribution transformer is

(a) at no load

(b) at 50% full load

(c) at 80% full load

(d) at full load

30. Transformer breaths in when

(a) load on it increases

(b) load on it decreases

(c) load remains constant

(d) none of the above

31. No-load current of a transformer has

(a) has high magnitude and low power factor

(b) has high magnitude and high power factor

(c) has small magnitude and high power factor

(d) has small magnitude and low power factor

32. Spacers are provided between adjacent coils

(a) to provide free passage to the cooling oil

(b) to insulate the coils from each other

(c) both (a) and (b)

(d) none of the above

33. Greater the secondary leakage flux

(a) less will be the secondary induced e.m.f.

(b) less will be the primary induced e.m.f.

(c) less will be the primary terminal voltage

(d) none of the above

34. The purpose of providing iron core in a step-up transformer is

(a) to provide coupling between primary and secondary

(b) to increase the magnitude of mutual flux

(c) <u>to decrease the magnitude of mag-netizing current</u>

(d) to provide all above features

35. The power transformer is a constant

(a) voltage device

(b) current device

(c) power device

(d) <u>main flux device</u>

36. Two transformers operating in parallel will share the load depending upon their

(a) leakage reactance

(b) <u>per unit impedance</u>

(c) efficiencies

(d) ratings

37. If R2 is the resistance of secondary winding of the transformer and K is the transformation ratio then the equivalent secondary resistance referred to primary will be

(a) R2/VK

(b) <u>R2IK2</u>

(c) R22!K2

(d) R22/K

38. What will happen if the transformers working in parallel are not connected with regard to polarity ?

(a) The power factor of the two trans-formers will be different from the power factor of common load

(b) <u>Incorrect polarity will result in dead short circuit</u>

(c) The transformers will not share load in proportion to their kVA ratings

(d) none of the above

39. If the percentage impedances of the two transformers working in parallel are different, then

(a) transformers will be overheated

(b) power factors of both the transformers will be same

(c) parallel operation will be not possible

(d) <u>parallel operation will still be possible, but the power factors at which the two transformers operate will be different from the power factor</u>

of the common load

40. In a transformer the tappings are generally provided on

(a) primary side

(b) secondary side

(c) low voltage side

(d) high voltage side

41. The use of higher flux density in the transformer design

(a) reduces weight per kVA

(6) reduces iron losses

(c) reduces copper losses

(d) increases part load efficiency

42. The chemical used in breather for transformer should have the quality of

(a) ionizing air

(b) absorbing moisture

(c) cleansing the transformer oil

(d) cooling the transformer oil.

43. The chemical used in breather is

(a) asbestos fiber

(b) silica sand

(c) sodium chloride

(d) silica gel

45. The transformer ratings are usually expressed in terms of

(a) volts

(b) amperes

(c) kW

(d) kVA

46. The noise resulting from vibrations of laminations set by magnetic forces, is termed as

(a) magnetostrication

(b) boo

(c) hum

(d) zoom

47. Hysteresis loss in a transformer varies as CBmax = maximum flux density)

(a) Bmax

(b) Bmax1-6

(C) Bmax1-83

(d) B max

48. Material used for construction of transformer core is usually

(a) wood

(b) copper

(c) aluminium

(d) <u>silicon steel</u>

49. The thickness of laminations used in a transformer is usually

(a) <u>0.4 mm to 0.5 mm</u>

(b) 4 mm to 5 mm

(c) 14 mm to 15 mm

(d) 25 mm to 40 mm

50. The function of conservator in a transformer is

(a) to project against'internal fault

(b) to reduce copper as well as core losses

(c) to cool the transformer oil

(d) <u>to take care of the expansion and contraction of transformer oil due to variation of temperature of sur-roundings</u>

51. The highest voltage for transmitting electrical power in India is

(a) 33 kV.

(6) 66 kV

(c) 132 kV

(d) <u>400 kV</u>

52. In a transformer the resistance between its primary and secondary is

(a) zero

(b) 1 ohm

(c) 1000 ohms

(d) <u>infinite</u>

53. A transformer oil must be free from

(a) sludge

(b) odour

(c) gases

(d) <u>moisture</u>

54. A Buchholz relay can be installed on

(a) auto-transformers

(b) air-cooled transformers

(c) welding transformers

(d) <u>oil cooled transformers</u>

55. Gas is usually not liberated due to dissociation of transformer oil unless the oil temperature exceeds
(a) 50°C
(b) 80°C
(c) 100°C
(d) <u>150°C</u>
56. The main reason for generation of harmonics in a transformer could be
(a) fluctuating load
(b) poor insulation
(c) mechanical vibrations
(d) <u>saturation of core</u>
57. Distribution transformers are generally designed for maximum efficiency around
(a) 90% load
(b) zero load
(c) 25% load
(d) <u>50% load</u>
58. Which of the following property is not necessarily desirable in the material for transformer core ?
(a) Mechanical strength
(6) Low hysteresis loss
(c) <u>High thermal conductivity</u>
(d) High permeability
59. Star/star transformers work satisfactorily when
(a) load is unbalanced only
(b) <u>load is balanced only</u>
(c) on balanced as well as unbalanced loads
(d) none of the above
60. Delta/star transformer works satisfactorily when
(a) load is balanced only
(b) load is unbalanced only
(c) <u>on balanced as well as unbalanced loads</u>
(d) none of the above
61. Buchholz's relay gives warning and protection against
(a) <u>electrical fault inside the transformer itself</u>
(b) electrical fault outside the transformer in outgoing feeder
(c) for both outside and inside faults

(d) none of the above

62. The magnetising current of a transformer is usually small because it has

(a) <u>small air gap</u>

(b) large leakage flux

(c) laminated silicon steel core

(d) fewer rotating parts

63. Which of the following does not change in an ordinary transformer ?

(a) <u>Frequency</u>

(b) Voltage

(c) Current

(d) Any of the above

64. Which of the following properties is not necessarily desirable for the material for transformer core ?

(a) Low hysteresis loss

(b) High permeability

(c) <u>High thermal conductivity</u>

(d) Adequate mechanical strength

65. The leakage flux in a transformer depends upon

(a) <u>load current</u>

(b) load current and voltage

(c) load current, voltage and frequency

(d) load current, voltage, frequency and power factor

66. The path of the magnetic flux in transformer should have

(a) high reluctance

(b) <u>low reactance</u>

(c) high resistance

(d) low resistance

67. Noise level test in a transformer is a

(a) special test

(b) routine test

(c) <u>type test</u>

(d) none of the above

68. Which of the following is not a routine test on transformers ?

(a) Core insulation voltage test

(b) Impedance test

(c) <u>Radio interference test</u>

(d) Polarity test

69. A transformer can have zero voltage regulation at

(a) <u>leading power factor</u>

(b) lagging power factor

(c) unity power factor

(d) zero power factor

70. Helical coils can be used on

(a) <u>low voltage side of high kVA transformers</u>

(b) high frequency transformers

(c) high voltage side of small capacity transformers

(d) high voltage side of high kVA rating transformers

1. A semiconductor is formed by .... bonds.

A] <u>Covalent</u>

B] Electrovalent

C] Co-ordinate

D] None of the above

2. A semiconductor has .... temperature coefficient of resistance.

A] Positive

B] Zero

C] <u>Negative</u>

D] None of the above

3. The most commonly used semiconductor is ....

A] Germanium

B] <u>Silicon</u>

C] Carbon

D] Sulphur

6. The resistivity of a pure silicon is about ....

A] 100 O cm

B] <u>6000 O cm</u>

C] 3 x 105 O m

D] 6 x 10-8 O cm

7. When a pure semiconductor is heated, its resistance ....

A] Goes up

B] <u>Goes down</u>

C] Remains the same

D] Can't say

8. The strength of a semiconductor crystal comes from ....

A] Forces between nuclei

B] Forces between protons

C] <u>Electron-pair bonds</u>

D] None of the above

9. When a pentavalent impurity is added to a pure semiconductor, it becomes ....

A] An insulator

B] An intrinsic semiconductor

C] p-type semiconductor

D] <u>n-type semiconductor</u>

10. Addition of pentavalent impurity to a semiconductor createsmany ....

A] <u>Free electrons</u>

B] Holes

C] Valence electrons

D] Bound electrons

11. A pentavalent impurity has .... Valence electrons

A] 35

B] <u>4</u>

C] 6

12. An n-type semiconductor is ....

A] Positively charged

B] Negatively charged

C] <u>Electrically neutral</u>

D] None of the above

14. Addition of trivalent impurity to a semiconductor creates many ....

A] <u>Holes</u>

B] Free electrons

C] Valence electrons

D] Bound electrons

15. A hole in a semiconductor is defined as ....

A] A free electron

B] <u>The incomplete part of an electron pair bond</u>

C] A free proton

D] A free neutron

16. The impurity level in an extrinsic semiconductor is about ..... of pure semiconductor.

A] 10 atoms for 108 atoms

B] <u>1 atom for 108 atoms</u>

C] 1 atom for 104 atoms

D] 1 atom for 100 atoms

17. As the doping to a pure semiconductor increases, the bulk resistance of the semiconductor ....

A] Remains the same

B] Increases

C] <u>Decreases</u>

D] None of the above

18. A hole and electron in close proximity would tend to ....

A] Repel each other

B] <u>Attract each other</u>

C] Have no effect on each other

D] None of the above

19. In a semiconductor, current conduction is due to ....

A] Only holes

B] Only free electrons

C] <u>Holes and free electrons</u>

D] None of the above

20. The random motion of holes and free electrons due to thermal agitation is called ....

A] <u>Diffusion</u>

B] Pressure

C] Ionisation

D] None of the above

21. A forward biased pn junction diode has a resistance of the order of

A] <u>Ωk</u>

B] O

C] MO

D] None of the above

22. The battery connections required to forward bias a pn junction are ......

A] <u>+ve terminal to p and −ve terminal to n</u>

B] -ve terminal to p and +ve terminal to n

C] -ve terminal to p and −ve terminal to n

D] None of the above

23. The barrier voltage at a pn junction for germanium is about ....

A] 5 V

B] 3 V

C] Zero

D] <u>3 V</u>

24. In the depletion region of a pn junction, there is a shortage of ....

A] Acceptor ions

B] <u>Holes and electrons</u>

C] Donor ions

D] None of the above

25. A reverse bias pn junction has ....

A] narrow depletion layer

B] <u>Almost no current</u>

C] Very low resistance

D] Large current flow

26. A pn junction acts as a ....

A] Controlled switch

B] Bidirectional switch

C] <u>Unidirectional switch</u>

D] None of the above

27. A reverse biased pn junction has resistance of the order of

A] Ok

B] O

C] <u>MO</u>

D] None of the above

28. The leakage current across a pn junction is due to ....

A] <u>Minority carriers</u>

B] Majority carriers

C] Junction capacitance

D] None of the above

29. When the temperature of an extrinsic semiconductor is increased, the pronounced effect is on......

A] Junction capacitance

B] <u>Minority carriers</u>

C] Majority carriers

D] None of the above

30. With forward bias to a pn junction , the width of depletion layer ....

A] <u>Decreases</u>

B] Increases

C] Remains the same

D] None of the above

31. The leakage current in a pn junction is of the order of

A] Aa

B] mA

C] kA

D] μA

32. In an intrinsic semiconductor, the number of free electrons ....

A] <u>Equals the number of holes</u>

B] Is greater than the number of holes

C] Is less than the number of holes

D] None of the above

33. At room temperature, an intrinsic semiconductor has ....

A] Many holes only

B] <u>A few free electrons and holes</u>

C] Many free electrons only

D] No holes or free electrons

34. At absolute temperature, an intrinsic semiconductor has ....

A] A few free electrons

B] Many holes

C] Many free electrons

D] <u>No holes or free electrons</u>

35. At room temperature, an intrinsic silicon crystal acts approximately as ......

A] A battery

B] A conductor

C] <u>An insulator</u>

D] A piece of copper wire

1. A crystal diode has ....

one pn junction

two pn junctions

three pn junctions

none of the above

ANS: 1

2. A crystal diode has forward resistance of the order of ....

kΩ

Ω

MΩ

none of the above

ANS: 2

3. If the arrow of crystal diode symbol is positive w.r.t. bar, then diode is .... biased.

forward

reverse

either forward or reverse

none of the above

ANS: 1

SEMICONDUCTOR DIODE

Questions and Answers pdf

4. The reverse current in a diode is of the order of ....

kA

mA

μA

A

ANS: 3

5. The forward voltage drop across a silicon diode is about ....

2.5 V

3 V

10 V

0.7 V

ANS: 4

6. A crystal diode is used as ....

an amplifier

a rectifier

an oscillator

a voltage regulator

ANS: 2

7. The d.c. resistance of a crystal diode is .... its a.c. resistance

the same as

more than

less than

none of the above

ANS: 3

8. An ideal crystal diode is one which behaves as a perfect .... when forward biased.

conductor

insulator

resistance material

none of the above

ANS: 1

9. The ratio of reverse resistance and forward resistance of a germanium crystal diode is about ....

1 : 1

100 : 1

1000 : 1

40,000 : 1

ANS: 4

10. The leakage current in a crystal diode is due to ....

minority carriers

majority carriers

junction capacitance

none of the above

ANS: 1

11. If the temperature of a crystal diode increases, then leakage current ....

remains the same

decreases

increases

becomes zero

ANS: 3

12. The PIV rating of a crystal diode is .... that of equivalent vacuum diode

the same as

lower than

more than

none of the above

ANS: 2

13. If the doping level of a crystal diode is increased, the breakdown voltage.............

remains the same

is increased

is decreased

none of the above

ANS: 3

14. The knee voltage of a crystal diode is approximately equal

to ....
applied voltage
breakdown voltage
forward voltage
barrier potential
ANS: 4
15. When the graph between current through and voltage across a device is a straight line, the device is referred to as ....
linear
active
nonlinear
passive
ANS: 1
16. When the crystal current diode current is large, the bias is ....
forward
inverse
poor
reverse
ANS: 1
17. A crystal diode is a .... device
non-linear
bilateral
linear
none of the above
ANS: 1
18. A crystal diode utilises .... characteristic for rectification
reverse
forward
forward or reverse
none of the above
ANS: 2
19. When a crystal diode is used as a rectifier, the most important consideration is ....
forward characteristic
doping level
reverse characteristic
PIC rating
ANS: 4

20. If the doping level in a crystal diode is increased, the width of depletion layer...........
remains the same
is decreased
in increased
none of the above
ANS: 3
21. A zener diode has ....
one pn junction
two pn junctions
three pn junctions
none of the above
ANS: 1
22. A zener diode is used as ....
an amplifier
a voltage regulator
a rectifier
a multivibrator
ANS: 2
23. The doping level in a zener diode is .... that of a crystal diode
the same as
less than
more than
none of the above
ANS: 3
24. A zener diode is always .... connected.
reverse
forward
either reverse or forward
none of the above
ANS: 1
25. A zener diode utilizes .... characteristics for its operation.
forward
reverse
both forward and reverse
none of the above
ANS: 2
26. In the breakdown region, a zener didoe behaves like a ....

source.

constant voltage

constant current

constant resistance

none of the above

ANS: 1

27. A zener diode is destroyed if it..............

is forward biased

is reverse biased

carrier more than rated current

none of the above

ANS: 3

28. A series resistance is connected in the zener circuit to...........

properly reverse bias the zener

protect the zener

properly forward bias the zener

none of the above

ANS: 2

29. A zener diode is .... device

a non-linear

a linear

an amplifying

none of the above

ANS: 1

30. A zener diode has .... breakdown voltage

undefined

sharp

zero

none of the above

ANS: 2

31. .... rectifier has the lowest forward resistance

solid state

vacuum tube

gas tube

none of the above

ANS: 1

32. Mains a.c. power is converrted into d.c. power for ....

lighting purposes

heaters

using in electronic equipment

none of the above

ANS: 3

33. The disadvantage of a half-wave rectifier is that the...................

components are expensive

diodes must have a higher power rating

output is difficult to filter

none of the above

ANS: 3

34. If the a.c. input to a half-wave rectifier is an r.m.s value of $400/\sqrt{2}$

volts, then diode PIV rating is ....

$400/\sqrt{2}$ V

400 V

400 x $\sqrt{2}$ V

none of the above

ANS: 2

35. The ripple factor of a half-wave rectifier is ....

21

.21

2.5

0.48

ANS: 4

36. There is a need of transformer for ....

half-wave rectifier

centre-tap full-wave rectifier

bridge full-wave rectifier

none of the above

ANS: 2

37. The PIV rating of each diode in a bridge rectifier is .... that

of the equivalent centre-tap rectifier

one-half

the same as

twice

four times

ANS: 1

38. For the same secondary voltage, the output voltage from a centretap

rectifier is .... than that of bridge rectifier

twice

thrice

four time

one-half

ANS: 4

39. If the PIV rating of a diode is exceeded, ...

the diode conducts poorly

the diode is destroyed

the diode behaves like a zener diode

none of the above

ANS: 2

40. A 10 V power supply would use .... as filter capacitor.

paper capacitor

mica capacitor

electrolytic capacitor

air capacitor

ANS: 3

41. A 1,000 V power supply would use .... as a filter capacitor

paper capacitor

air capacitor

mica capacitor

electrolytic capacitor

ANS: 1

42. The .... filter circuit results in the best voltage regulation

choke input

capacitor input

resistance input

none of the above

ANS: 1

43. A half-wave rectifier has an input voltage of 240 V r.m.s. If the step-down transformer has a turns ratio of 8:1, what is the peak load voltage? Ignore diode drop.

27.5 V

86.5 V

30 V

42.5 V

ANS: 4

44. The maximum efficiency of a half-wave rectifier is ....

40.6 %

81.2 %

50 %

25 %

ANS: 1

45. The most widely used rectifier is ....

half-wave rectifier

centre-tap full-wave rectifier

bridge full-wave rectifier

none of the above

ANS:3

1. A transistor has ....

A] one pn junction

B] two pn junctions

C] three pn junctions

D] four pn junctions

2. The number of depletion layers in a transistor is ....

A] four

B] three

C] one

D] two

3. The base of a transistor is .... doped

A] heavily

B] moderately

C] lightly

D] none of the above

4. The element that has the biggest size in a transistor is ....

A] collector

B] base

C] emitter

D] collector-base-junction

5. In a pnp transistor, the current carriers are ....

A] acceptor ions

B] donor ions

C] free electrons

D] holes

6. The collector of a transistor is .... doped

A] heavily

B] <u>moderately</u>

C] lightly

D] none of the above

7. A transistor is a .... operated device

A] <u>current</u>

B] voltage

C] both voltage and current

D] none of the above

8. In a npn transistor, ... are the minority carriers

A] free electrons

B] <u>holes</u>

C] donor ions

D] acceptor ions

9. The emitter of a transistor is .... doped

A] lightly

B] <u>heavily</u>

C] moderately

D] none of the above

10. In a transistor, the base current is about .... of emitter current

A] 25%

B] 20%

C] 35 %

D] <u>5%</u>

11. At the base-emitter junctions of a transistor, one finds ....

A] a reverse bias

B] a wide depletion layer

C] <u>low resistance</u>

D] none of the above

12. The input impedance of a transistor is ....

A] high

B] <u>low</u>

C] very high

D] almost zero

13. Most of the majority carriers from the emitter ....

A] recombine in the base

B] recombine in the emitter

C] <u>pass through the base region to the collector</u>

D] none of the above

14. The current IB is ....
A] electron current
B] hole current
C] donor ion current
D] acceptor ion current

15. In a transistor ....
A] IC = IE + IB
B] IB = IC + IE
C] IE = IC – IB
D] IE = IC + IB

16. The value of a of a transistor is ....
A] more than 1
B] less than 1
C] 1
D] none of the above

17. IC = aIE + ...
A] IB
B] ICEO
C] ICBO
D] ßIB

18. The output impedance of a transistor is ....
A] high
B] zero
C] low
D] very low

19. In a tansistor, IC = 100 mA and IE = 100.2 mA. The value of ß is
....
A] 100
B] 50
C] about 1
D] 200

20. In a transistor if ß = 100 and collector current is 10 mA, then IE
is ....
A] 100 mA
B] 100.1 mA
C] 110 mA
D] none of the above

21. The relation between ß and a is ....

A] ß = 1 / (1 – a)

B] ß = (1 – a) / a

C] ß = a / (1 – a)

D] ß = a / (1 + a)

22. The value of ß for a transistor is generally ....

A] 1less than 1

B] between 20 and 500

C] above 500

23. The most commonly used transistor arrangement is .... arrangement

A] common emitter

B] common base

C] common collector

D] none of the above

24. The input impedance of a transistor connected in ....arrangement is the highest

A] common emitter

B] common collector

C] common base

D] none of the above

25. The output impedance of a transistor connected in ....

A] arrangement is the highest

B] common emitter

C] common collector

D] common base

none of the above

26. The phase difference between the input and output voltages in a common base arrangement is ....

A] 180o

B] 90o

C] 270o

D] 0o

27. The power gain in a transistor connected in .... arrangement is the highest

A] common emitter

B] common base

C] common collector

D] none of the above

28. The phase difference between the input and output voltages of a transistor connected in common emitter arrangement is ....

A] 0o

B] <u>180o</u>

C] 90o

D] 270o

29. The voltage gain in a transistor connected in .... arrangement is the highest

A] common base

B] common collector

C] <u>common emitter</u>

D] none of the above

30. As the temperature of a transistor goes up, the base-emitter resistance ....

A] <u>decreases</u>

B] increases

C] remains the same

D] none of the above

31. The voltage gain of a transistor connected in common collector

A] arrangement is ....

B] equal to 1

C] more than 10

D] <u>more than 100 less than 1</u>

32. The phase difference between the input and output voltages of a transistor connected in common collector arrangement is ....

A] 180o

B] <u>0o</u>

C] 90o

D] 270o

33. $IC = ß \ IB + $ ....

A] ICBO

B] IC

C] <u>ICEO</u>

D] aIE

34. $IC = [a / (1 - a)] \ IB + $ ....

A] <u>ICEO</u>

B] ICBO

C] IC

D] (1 – a) IB

35. IC = [a / (1 – a)] IB + [........ / (1 – a)]

A] ICBO

B] ICEO

C] IC

D] IE

36. BC 147 transistor indicates that it is made of ....

A] germanium

B] silicon

C] carbon

D] none of the above

37. ICEO = (.........) ICBO

A] ß1

B] + a

C] 1 + ß

D] none of the above

38. A transistor is connected in CB mode. If it is not connected in CE mode with same bias voltages, the values of IE, IB and IC will ....

A] remain the same

B] increase

C] decrease

D] none of the above

39. If the value of a is 0.9, then value of ß is ....

A] 9

B] 0.9

C] 900

D] 90

40. In a transistor, signal is transferred from a .... circuit

A] high resistance to low resistance

B] low resistance to high resistance

C] high resistance to high resistance

D] low resistance to low resistance

41. The arrow in the symbol of a transistor indicates the direction of ....

A] electron current in the emitter

B] electron current in the collector

C] hole current in the emitter

D] donor ion current

42. The leakage current in CE arrangement is .... that in CB arrangement

A] <u>more than</u>

B] less than

C] the same as

D] none of the above

43. A heat sink is generally used with a transistor to ....

A] increase the forward current

B] decrease the forward current

C] compensate for excessive doping

D] <u>prevent excessive temperature rise</u>

44. The most commonly used semiconductor in the manufacture of a transistor is ....

A] germanium

B] <u>silicon</u>

C] carbon

D] none of the above

45. The collector-base junction in a transistor has ....

A] forward bias at all times

B] <u>reverse bias at all times</u>

C] low resistance

D] none of the above

1. Transistor biasing represents .... conditions

1. a.c.

2. d.c.

3. both a.c. and d.c.

4. none of the above

Ans : 2

2. Transistor biasing is done to keep .... in the circuit

Proper direct current

Proper alternating current

The base current small

Collector current small

Ans : 1

3. Operating point represents ....

Values of IC and VCE when signal is applied

The magnitude of signal

Zero signal values of IC and VCE

None of the above

Ans : 3

TRANSISTOR BIASING Questions and Answers pdf

4. If biasing is not done in an amplifier circuit, it results in ....

Decrease in the base current

Unfaithful amplification

Excessive collector bias

None of the above

Ans : 2

5. Transistor biasing is generally provided by a ....

Biasing circuit

Bias battery

Diode

None of the above

Ans : 1

6. For faithful amplification by a transistor circuit, the value of VBE should .... for a silicon transistor

Be zero

Be 0.01 V

Not fall below 0.7 V

Be between 0 V and 0.1 V

Ans : 3

7. For proper operation of the transistor, its collector should have ....

Proper forward bias

Proper reverse bias

Very small size

None of the above

Ans : 2

8. For faithful amplification by a transistor circuit, the value of VCE should .... for silicon transistor

Not fall below 1 V

Be zero

Be 0.2 V

None of the above

Ans : 1

9. The circuit that provides the best stabilization of operating point is ....

Base resistor bias

Collector feedback bias

Potential divider bias

None of the above

Ans : 3

10. The point of intersection of d.c. and a.c. load lines represents ....

Operating point

Current gain

Voltage gain

None of the above

Ans : 1

11. An ideal value of stability factor is ....

100

200

More than 200

1

Ans : 4

12. The zero signal IC is generally .... mA in the initial stages of a transistor amplifier

41

3

More than 10

Ans : 2

13. If the maximum collector current due to signal alone is 3 mA, then zero signal collector current should be at least equal to ....

6 mA

mA

3 mA

1 mA

Ans : 3

14. The disadvantage of base resistor method of transistor biasing is that it ....

Is complicated

Is sensitive to changes in ß

Provides high stability

None of the above

Ans : 2

15. The biasing circuit has a stability factor of 50. If due to temperature change, ICBO changes by 1 μA, then IC will change by ....

100 μA

25 μA

20 μA

50 μA

Ans : 4

16. For good stabilsation in voltage divider bias, the current I1 flowing through R1 and R2 should be equal to or greater than

10 IB

3 IB

2 IB

4 IB

Ans : 1

17. The leakage current in a silicon transistor is about .... the leakage current in a germanium transistor

One hundredth

One tenth

One thousandth

One millionth

Ans : 3

18. The operating point is also called the ....

Cut off point

Quiescent point

Saturation point

None of the above

Ans : 2

19. For proper amplification by a transistor circuit, the operating point should be located at the .... of the d.c. load line

The end point

Middle

The maximum current point

None of the above

Ans : 2

20. The operating point .... on the a.c. load line

Also line

Does not lie

May or may not lie

Data insufficient

Ans : 1

21. The disadvantage of voltage divider bias is that it has ....

High stability factor

Low base current

Many resistors

None of the above

Ans : 3

22. Thermal runaway occurs when ....

Collector is reverse biased

Transistor is not biased

Emitter is forward biased

Junction capacitance is high

Ans : 2

23. The purpose of resistance in the emitter circuit of a transistor amplifier is to ....

Limit the maximum emitter current

Provide base-emitter bias

Limit the change in emitter current

None of the above

Ans : 3

24. In a transistor amplifier circuit VCE = VCB + ...

VBE

2VBE

5 VBE

None of the above

Ans : 1

25. The base resistor method is generally used in ....

Amplifier circuits

Switching circuits

Rectifier circuits

None of the above

Ans : 2

26. For germanium transistor amplifier, VCE should .... for faithful amplification

Be zero

Be 0.2 V

Not fall below 0.7 V

None of the above

Ans : 3

27. In a base resistor method, if the value of ß changes by 50, then collector current will change by a factor ....

25

50

100

200

Ans : 2

28. The stability factor of a collector feedback bias circuit is .... that of base resistor bias.

The same as

More than

Less than

None of the above

Ans : 3

29. In the design of a biasing circuit, the value of collector load RC is determined by ....

VCE consideration

VBE consideration

IB consideration

None of the above

Ans : 1

30. If the value of collector current IC increases, then the value of VCE ....

Remains the same

Decreases

Increases

None of the above

Ans : 2

31. If the temperature increases, the value of VCE ....

Remains the same

Is increased

Is decreased

None of the above

Ans : 3

32. The stabilisation of operating point in potential divider method is provided by ....

RE consideration

RC consideration

VCC consideration

None of the above

Answer: 1

33. The value of VBE ....

Depends upon IC to moderate extent

Is almost independent of IC

Is strongly dependant on IC

None of the above

Ans : 2

34. When the temperature changes, the operating point is shifted due to ....

Change in ICBO

Change in VCC

Change in the values of circuit resistance

None of the above

Ans : 1

35. The value of stability factor for a base resistor bias is ....

RB (ß+1)

(ß+1)RC

(ß+1)

1-ß

Ans : 3

36. In a particular biasing circuit, the value of RE is about ....

10 kO

1 MO

100 kO

800 O

Ans : 4

37. A silicon transistor is biased with base resistor method. If ß=100, VBE =0.7 V, zero signal collector current IC = 1 mA and VCC = 6V , what is the value of the base resistor RB?

105 kO

530 kO

315 kO

None of the above

Ans : 2

38. In voltage divider bias, VCC = 25 V; R1 = 10 kO; R2 = 2.2 V ; RC = 3.6 V and RE =1 kO. What is the emitter voltage?

7 V

3 V

V8

V

Ans : 4

39. In the above question (Q38.) , what is the collector voltage?

3 V

8 V

6 V

7 V

Ans : 1

40. In voltage divider bias, operating point is 3 V, 2 mA. If VCC = 9 V, RC = 2.2 kO, what is the value of RE ?

2000 O

1400 O

800 O

1600 O

Ans : 3

1. Which of the following are the applications of D.C. system ?

(a) Battery charging work

(b) Arc welding

(c) Electrolytic and electro-chemical processes

(d) Arc lamps for search lights

(e) All of the above

Ans: e

2. Which of the following methods may be used to convert A.C. system to D.C. ?

(a) Rectifiers

(b) Motor converters

(c) Motor-generator sets

(d) Rotary converters

(e) All of the above

Ans: e

3. In a single phase rotary converter the number of slip rings will be

(a) two
(b) three
(c) four
(d) six
(e) none
Ans: a
4. A synchronous converter can be started
(a) by means of a small auxiliary motor
(b) from AC. side as induction motor
(c) from D.C. side as D.C. motor
(d) any of the above methods
(e) none of the above methods
Ans: d
5. A rotary converter is a single machine with
(a) one armature and one field
(b) two armatures and one field
(c) one armature and two fields
(d) none of the above
Ans: a
6. A rotary converter combines the function of
(a) an induction motor and a D.C. generator
(b) a synchronous motor and a D.C. generator.
(c) a D.C. series motor and a D.C. generator
(d) none of the above
Ans: b
7. Which of the following is reversible in action ?
(a) Motor generator set
(b) Motor converter
(c) Rotary converter
(d) Any of the above
(e) None of the above
Ans: c
8. Which of the following metals is generally manufactured by electrolysis
process ?
(a) Load
(b) Aluminium
(c) Copper

(d) Zinc

(e) None of the above

Ans: b

9. With a motor converter it is possible to obtain D.C. voltage only upto

(a) 200-100 V

(6) 600—800 V

(c) 1000—1200 V

(d) 1700—2000 V

Ans: d

10. Normally, which of the following is used, when a large-scale conversion from

AC. to D.C. power is required ?

(a) Motor-generator set

(b) Motor converter

(c) Rotary converter

(d) Mercury arc rectifier

Ans: d

11. A rotary converter in general construction and design, is more or less like

(a) a transformer

(b) an induction motor

(c) an alternator

(d) any D.C. machine

Ans: d

12. A rotary converter operates at a

(a) low power factor

(6) high power factor

(c) zero power factor

(d) none of the above

Ans: b

13. In which of the following appUcations, direct current is absolutely essential ?

(a) Illumination

(b) Electrolysis

(c) Variable speed operation

(d) Traction

Ans: b

14. Which of the following AC. motors is usually used in large motor-generator
sets?
(a) Synchronous motor
(b) Squirrel cage induction motor
(c) Slip ring induction motor
(d) Any of the above
Ans: a

15. In a rotary converter armature currents are
(a) d.c. only
(b) a.c. only
(c) partly a.c. and partly d.c.
Ans: c

16. In which of the following equipment direct current is needed ?
(a) Telephones
(b) Relays
(c) Time switches
(d) All of the above
Ans: d

17. In a rotary converter I2R losses as compared to a D.C. generator of
the same
size will be
(a) same
(b) less
(c) double
(d) three times
Ans: b

18. In a mercury arc rectifier positive ions are attracted towards
(a) anode
(b) cathode
(c) shell bottom
(d) mercury pool
Ans: b

19. Mercury, in arc rectifiers, is chosen for cathode because
(a) its ionization potential is relatively low
(b) its atomic weight is quite high
(c) its boiling point and specific heat are low
(d) it remains in liquid state at ordi¬nary temperature

(e) all of the above

Ans: e

20. The ionization potential of mercury is approximately

(a) 5.4 V

(b) 8.4 V

(c) 10.4 V

(d) 16.4 V

Ans: c

21. The potential drop in the arc, in a mercury arc rectifier, varies

(a) 0.05 V to 0.2 V per cm length of the arc

(b) 0.5 V to 1.5 V per cm length of the arc

(c) 2 V to 3.5 V per cm length of the arc

(d) none of the above

Ans: d

22. The voltage drop between the anode and cathode, of a mercury arc rectifier

comprises of the following

(a) anode drop and cathode drop

(b) anode drop and arc drop

(c) cathode drop and arc drop

(d) anode drop, cathode drop and arc drop

Ans: d

23. Glass rectifiers are usually made into units capable of D.C. output (maximum

continuous rating) of

(a) 100 A at 100 V

(b) 200 A at 200 V

(c) 300 A at 300 V

(d) 400 A at 400 V

(e) 500 A at 500 V

Ans: e

24. The voltage drop at anode, in a mercury arc rectifier is due to

(a) self restoring property of mercury

(b) high ionization potential

(c) energy spent in overcoming the electrostatic field

(d) high temperature inside the rectifier

Ans: c

25. The internal efficiency of a mercury arc rectifier depends on

(a) voltage only
(b) current only
(c) voltage and current
(d) r.m.s. value of current
(e) none of the above
Ans: a

26. If cathode and anode connections in a mercury arc rectifier are inter changed
(a) the rectifier will not operate
(b) internal losses will be reduced
(c) both ion and electron streams will move in the same direction
(d) the rectifier will operate at reduced efficiency
Ans: a

27. The cathdde voltage drop, in a mercury arc rectifier, is due to
(a) expenditure of energy in ionization
(b) surface resistance
(c) expenditure of energy in overcoming the electrostatic field
(d) expenditure of energy in liberating electrons from the mercury
Ans: d

28. To produce cathode spot in a mercury arc rectifier
(a) anode is heated
(b) tube is evacuated
(c) an auxiliary electrode is used
(d) low mercury vapour pressures are used
Ans: c

29. The advantage of mercury arc rectifier is that
(a) it is light in weight and occupies small floor space
(b) it has high efficiency
(c) it has high overload capacity
(d) it is comparatively noiseless
(e) all of the above
Ans: e

30. In a mercury pool rectifier, the voltage drop across its electrodes
(a) is directly proportional to load
(b) is inversely proportional to load
(c) varies exponentially with the load current
(d) is almost independent of load current
Ans: d

RECTIFIERS & CONVERTERS – Electrical Engineering Interview Questions

and Answers

31. In a three-phase mercury arc rectifiers each anode conducts for

(a) one-third of a cycle

(b) one-fourth of a cycle

(c) one-half a cycle

(d) two-third of a cycle

Ans: a

32. In a mercury arc rectifier characteristic blue luminosity is due to

(a) colour of mercury

(b) ionization

(c) high temperature

(d) electron streams

Ans: b

33. Which of the following mercury arc rectifier will deliver least undulating

current?

(a) Six-phase

(b) Three-phase

(c) Two-phase

(d) Single-phase

Ans: a

34. In a glass bulb mercury arc rectifier the maximum current rating is restricted

to

(a) 2000 A

(b) 1500 A

(c) 1000 A

(d) 500 A

Ans: d

35. In a mercury arc rectifier_______ flow from anode to cathode

(a) ions

(b) electrons

(c) ions and electrons

(d) any of the above

Ans: a

36. When a rectifier is loaded which of the following voltage drops take place ?

(a) Voltage drop in transformer reactance

(6) Voltage drop in resistance of transformer and smoothing chokes

(c) Arc voltage drop

(d) All of the above

Ans: d

37. On which of the following factors the number of phases for which a rectifier

should be designed depend ?

(a) The voltage regulation of the rec¬tifier should be low

(b) In the output circuit there should be no harmonics

(c) The power factor of the system should be high

(d) The rectifier supply transformer should be utilized to the best advantage

(e) all of the above

Ans: e

38. A mercury arc rectifier possesses _________ regulation characteristics

(a) straight line

(b) curved line

(c) exponential

(d) none of the above

Ans: d

39. It is the________of the transformer on which the magnitude of angle of

overlap depends.

(a) resistance

(b) capacitance

(c) leakage reactance

(d) any of the above

Ans: c

41. In a grid control of mercury arc rectifiers when the grid is made positive

relative to cathode, then it the electrons on their may to anode.

(a) accelerates

(b) decelerates

(c) any of the above

(d) none of the above

Ans: a

42. In mercury arc rectifiers having grid, the arc can be struck between anode and

cathode only when the grid attains a certain potential, this potential being known

as

(a) maximum grid voltage

(b) critical grid voltage

(c) any of the above

(d) none of the above

Ans: b

43. In phase-shift control method the control is carried out by varying the of grid

voltage.

(a) magnitude

(b) polarity

(c) phase

(d) any of the above

(e) none of the above

Ans: c

16.44. In a phase-shift control method, the phase shift between anode and grid

voltages can be achieved by means of

(a) shunt motor

(6) synchronous motor

(c) induction regulator

(d) synchronous generator

Ans: c

45. The metal rectifiers are preferred to valve rectifiers due to which of the

following advantages ?

(a) They are mechanically strong

(b) They do not require any voltage for filament heating

(c) Both (a) and (b)

(d) None of the above

Ans: c

46. Which of the following statement is incorrect ?

(a) Copper oxide rectifier is a linear device

(b) Copper oxide rectifier is not a perfect rectifier

(c) Copper oxide rectifier has a low efficiency

(d) Copper oxide rectifier finds use in control circuits

(e) Copper oxide rectifier is not stable during early life

Ans: a

47. The efficiency of the copper oxide rectifier seldom exceeds

(a) 90 to 95%

(b) 85 to 90%

(c) 80 to 85%

(d) 65 to 75%

Ans: d

48. Copper oxide rectifier is usually designed not to operate above

(a) 10°C

(b) 20°C

(c) 30°C

(d) 45°C

Ans: d

49. Selenium rectifier can be operated at temperatures as high as

(a) 25°C

(b) 40°C

(c) 60°C

(d) 75°C

Ans: d

50. In selenium rectifiers efficiencies ranging from _______ to _______ percent
are attainable

(a) 25, 35

(b) 40, 50

(c) 60, 70

(d) 75, 85

Ans: d

51. Ageing of a selenium rectifier may change the output voltage by

(a) 5 to 10 per cent

(b) 15 to 20 per cent

(c) 25 to 30 per cent

(d) none of the above

Ans: a

52. The applications of selenium rectifiers are usually limited to potential of

(a) 10 V

(b) 30 V

(c) 60 V

(d) 100 V

(e) 200 V

Ans: d

53. Which of the following rectifiers have been used extensively in supplying

direct current for electroplating ?

(a) Copper oxide rectifiers

(b) Selenium rectifiers

(c) Mercury arc rectifiers

(d) Mechanical rectifiers

(e) None of the above

Ans: b

54. A commutating rectifier consists of commutator driven by

(a) an induction motor

(b) a synchronous motor

(c) a D.C. series motor

(d) a D.C. shunt motor

Ans: b

55. Which of the following rectifiers are primarily used for charging of low voltage

batteries from AC. supply ?

(a) Mechanical rectifiers

(b) Copper oxide rectifiers

(c) Selenium rectifiers

(d) Electrolytic rectifiers

(e) Mercury arc rectifiers

Ans: d

56. The efficiency of an electrolytic rectifier is nearly

(a) 80%

(b) 70%

(c) 60%

(d) 40%

Ans: c

57. Which of the following is the loss within the mercury arc rectifier chamber ?

(a) Voltage drop in arc

(6) Voltage drop at the anode

(c) Voltage drop at the cathode

(d) All of the above

Ans: d

58. The metal rectifiers, as compared to mercury arc rectifiers

(a) operate on low temperatures

(b) can operate on high voltages

(c) can operate on heavy loads

(d) give poor regulation

(e) none of the above

Ans: a

59. In a mercury arc rectifier, the anode is usually made of

(a) copper

(b) aluminium

(c) silver

(d) graphite

(e) tungsten

Ans: d

1. A tuned amplifier uses .... load

A] Resistive

B] Capacitive

C] LC tank

D] Inductive

2. A tuned amplifier is generally operated in .... operation

A] Class A

B] Class C

C] Class B

D] None of the above

3. A tuned amplifier is used in .... applications

A] Radio frequency

B] Low frequency

C] Audio frequency

D] None of the above

4. Frequencies above .... kHz are called radio frequencies

A] 21

B] 0

C] 50

D] 200

6. The voltage gain of a tuned amplifier is .... at resonant frequency

A] Minimum

B] Maximum

C] Half-way between maximum and minimum

D] Zero

7. At parallel resonance, the line current is ....

A] Minimum

B] Maximum

C] Quite large

D] None of the above

8. At series resonance, the circuit offers .... impedance

A] Zero

B] Maximum

C] Minimum

D] None of the above

9. A resonant circuit contains .... elements

A] R and L only

B] R and C only

C] Only R

D] L and C

10. At series or parallel resonance, the circuit behaves as a .... load

A] Capacitive

B] Resistive

C] Inductive

D] None of the above

11. At series resonance, voltage across L is .... voltage across C

A] Equal to but opposite in phase to

B] Equal to but in phase with

C] Greater than but in phase with

D] Less than but in phase with

12. When either L or C is increased, the resonant frequency of LC circuit ....

A] Remains the same

B] Increases

C] Decreases

D] Insufficient data

13. At parallel resonance, the net reactive component circuit current is ....

A] Capacitive

B] <u>Zero</u>

C] Inductive

D] None of the above

14. In parallel resonance, the circuit impedance is ....

A] C/LR

B] R/LC

C] CR/L

D] <u>L/CR</u>

15. In a parallel LC circuit, if the input signal frequency is increased above resonant frequency then ....

A] <u>XL increases and XC decreases</u>

B] XL decreases and XC increases

C] Both XL and XC increase

D] Both XL and XC decrease

16. The Q of an LC circuit is given by ....

A] 2pfr x R

B] R / 2pfrL

C] <u>2pfrL / R</u>

D] R2/2pfrL

17. If Q of an LC circuit increases, then bandwidth ....

A] Increases

B] <u>Decreases</u>

C] Remains the same

D] Insufficient data

18. At series resonance, the net reactive component of circuit current is ....

A] <u>Zero</u>

B] Inductive

C] Capacitive

D] None of the above

19. The dimensions of L/CR are that of ....

A] Farad

B] Henry

C] <u>Ohm</u>

D] None of the above

20. If L/C ratio of a parallel LC circuit is increased, the Q of the circuit ....

A] Is decreased

B] <u>Is increased</u>

C] Remains the same

D] None of the above

21. At series resonance, the phase angle between applied voltage and circuit is ....

A] 90o

B] 180o

C] <u>0o</u>

D] None of the above

22. At parallel resonance, the ratio L/C is ....

A] <u>Very large</u>

B] Zero

C] Small

D] None of the above

23. If the resistance of a tuned circuit is increased, the Q of the circuit ....

A] Is increased

B] <u>Is decreased</u>

C] Remains the same

D] None of the above

24. The Q of a tuned circuit refers to the property of ....

A] Sensitivity

B] Fidelity

C] <u>Selectivity</u>

D] None of the above

25. At parallel resonance, the phase angle between the applied voltage and circuit current is ....

A] 90o

B] 180o

C] <u>0o</u>

D] None of the above

26. In a parallel LC circuit, if the signal frequency is decreased below the resonant frequency, then ....

A] <u>XL decreases and XC increases</u>

B] XL increases and XC decreases

C] Line current becomes minimum

D] None of the above

27. In series resonance, there is ....

A] <u>Voltage amplification</u>

B] Current amplification

C] Both voltage and current amplification

D] None of the above

28. The Q of a tuned amplifier is generally ....

A] Less than 5

B] Less than 10

C] <u>More than 10</u>

D] None of the above

29. The Q of a tuned amplifier is 50. If the resonant frequency for the amplifier is 1000kHZ, then bandwidth is ....

A] 10kHz

B] 40 kHz

C] 30 kHz

D] <u>20 kHz</u>

30. In the above question, what are the values of cut-off frequencies?

A] 140 kHz , 60 kHz

B] <u>1020 kHz , 980 kHz</u>

C] 1030 kHz , 970 kHz

D] None of the above

31. For frequencies above the resonant frequency, a parallel LC circuit behaves as a .... load

A] <u>Capacitive</u>

B] Resistive

C] Inductive

D] None of the above

32. In parallel resonance, there is ....

A] Both voltage and current amplification

B] Voltage amplifications

C] <u>Current amplification</u>

D] None of the above

33. For frequencies below resonant frequency, a series LC circuit behaves as a .... load

A] Resistive

B] <u>Capacitive</u>

C] Inductive

D] None of the above

34. If a high degree of selectivity is desired, then double-tuned circuit should have .... coupling

A] <u>Loose</u>

B] Tight

C] Critical

D] None of the above

35. In the double tuned circuit, if the mutual inductance between the two tuned circuits is decreased, the level of resonance curve ....

A] Remains the same

B] Is lowered

C] <u>Is raised</u>

D] None of the above

36. For frequencies above the resonant frequency , a series LC circuit behaves as a .... load

A] Resistive

B] <u>Inductive</u>

C] Capacitive

D] None of the above

37. Double tuned circuits are used in .... stages of a radio receiver

A] <u>IF</u>

B] Audio

C] Output

D] None of the above

38. A class C amplifier always drives .... load

A] A pure resistive

B] A pure inductive

C] A pure capacitive

D] <u>A resonant tank</u>

39. Tuned class C amplifiers are used for RF signals of ....

A] Low power

B] High power

C] Very high power

D] <u>None of the above</u>

40. For frequencies below the resonant frequency , a parallel LC circuit behaves as a .... load

A] <u>Inductive</u>
B] Resistive
C] Capacitive
D] None of the above
1. A radio receiver has .... of amplification
A] One stage
B] Two stages
C] Three stages
D] <u>More than one stages</u>
2. RC coupling is used for .... amplification
A] <u>Voltage</u>
B] Current
C] Power
D] None of the above
3. In an RC coupled amplifier, the voltage gain over mid-frequency range
....
A] Changes abruptly with frequency
B] <u>Is constant</u>
C] Changes uniformly with frequency
D] None of the above
4. In obtaining the frequency response curve of an amplifier, the ....
A] Amplifier level output is kept constant
B] Amplifier frequency is held constant
C] Generator frequency is held constant
D] <u>Generator output level is held constant</u>
5. An advantage of RC coupling scheme is the ....Good impedance matching
A] Economy
B] <u>High efficiency</u>
C] None of the above
6. The best frequency response is of .... coupling
A] RC
B] Transformer
C] <u>Direct</u>
D] None of the above
7. Transformer coupling is used for .... amplification
A] <u>Power</u>
B] Voltage

C] Current

D] None of the above

8. In an RC coupling scheme, the coupling capacitor CC must be large enough ....

A] To pass d.c. between the stages

B] <u>Not to attenuate the low frequencies</u>

C] To dissipate high power

D] None of the above

9. In RC coupling, the value of coupling capacitor is about ....

A] 100 pF

B] 0.1 μF

C] 0.01 μF

D] <u>10 μF</u>

11. When a multistage amplifier is to amplify d.c. signal, then one must use .... coupling

A] RC

B] Transformer

C] <u>Direct</u>

D] None of the above

12. .... coupling provides the maximum voltage gain

A] RC

B] <u>Transformer</u>

C] Direct

D] Impedance

13. In practice, voltage gain is expressed ....

A] <u>In db</u>

B] In volts

C] As a number

D] None of the above

14. Transformer coupling provides high efficiency because ....

A] Collector voltage is stepped up

B] <u>resistance is low</u>

C] collector voltage is stepped down

D] none of the above

15. Transformer coupling is generally employed when load resistance is ....

A] Large

B] Very large

C] <u>Small</u>

D] None of the above

16. If a three-stage amplifier has individual stage gains of 10 db, 5 db and 12 db, then total gain in db is ....

A] 600 db

B] 24 db

C] 14 db

D] <u>27 db</u>

17. The final stage of a multistage amplifier uses ....

A] RC coupling

B] <u>Transformer coupling</u>

C] Direct coupling

D] Impedance coupling

18. The ear is not sensitive to ....

A] <u>Frequency distortion</u>

B] Amplitude distortion

C] Frequency as well as amplitude distortion

D] None of the above

19. RC coupling is not used to amplify extremely low frequencies because ....

A] There is considerable power loss

B] There is hum in the output

C] <u>Electrical size of coupling capacitor becomes very large</u>

D] None of the above

20. In transistor amplifiers, we use .... transformer for impedance matching

A] Step up

B] <u>Step down</u>

C] Same turn ratio

D] None of the above

21. The lower and upper cut off frequencies are also called ....
frequencies

A] Sideband

B] Resonant

C] Half-resonant

D] <u>Half-power</u>

22. A gain of 1,000,000 times in power is expressed by ....

A] 30 db

B] <u>60 db</u>

C] 120 db

D] 600 db

23. A gain of 1000 times in voltage is expressed by ....

A] <u>60 db</u>

B] 30 db

C] 120 db

D] 600 db

24. 1 db corresponds to .... change in power level

A] 50%

B] 35%

C] <u>26%</u>

D] 22%

25. 1 db corresponds to .... change in voltage or current level

A] <u>40%</u>

B] 80%

C] 20%

D] 25%

26. The frequency response of transformer coupling is ....

A] Good

B] Very good

C] Excellent

D] <u>Poor</u>

27. In the initial stages of a multistage amplifier, we use ....

A] <u>RC coupling</u>

B] Transformer coupling

C] Direct coupling

D] None of the above

28. The total gain of a multistage amplifier is less than the product of the gains of individual stages due to ....

A] Power loss in the coupling device

B] <u>Loading effect of the next stage</u>

C] The use of many transistors

D] The use of many capacitors

29. The gain of an amplifier is expressed in db because ....

A] It is a simple unit

B] Calculations become easy

C] <u>Human ear response is logarithmic</u>

D] None of the above

30. If the power level of an amplifier reduces to half, the db gain will fall by ....

A] 5 db

B] 2 db

C] 10 db

D] 3 db

31. A current amplification of 2000 is a gain of ....

A] 3 db

B] 66 db

C] 20 db

D] 200 db

32. An amplifier receives 0.1 W of input signal and delivers 15 W of signal power. What is the power gain in db?

A] 8 db

B] 6 db

C] 5 db

D] 4 db

33. The power output of an audio system is 18 W. For a person to notice an increase in the output (loudness or sound intensity) of the system, what must the output power be increased to ?

A] 2 W

B] 6 W

C] 68 W

D] None of the above

34. The output of a microphone is rated at -52 db. The reference level is 1V under specified conditions. What is the output voltage of this microphone under the same sound conditions?

A] 5 mV

B] 2 mV

C] 8 mV

D] 5 mV

35. RC coupling is generally confined to low power applications because of ....

A] Large value of coupling capacitor

B] Low efficiency

C] Large number of components

D] None of the above

36. The number of stages that can be directly coupled is limited because ....

A] <u>Changes in temperature cause thermal instability</u>

B] Circuit becomes heavy and costly

C] It becomes difficult to bias the circuit

D] None of the above

37. The purpose of RC or transformer coupling is to ....

A] Block a.c.

B] <u>Separate bias of one stage from another</u>

C] Increase thermal stability

D] None of the above

38. The upper or lower cut off frequency is also called ....frequency

A] Resonant

B] Sideband

C] <u>3 db</u>

D] None of the above

39. The bandwidth of a single stage amplifier is .... that of a multistage amplifier

A] <u>More than</u>

B] The same as

C] Less than

D] Data insufficient

40. The value of emitter capacitor CE in a multistage amplifier is about ....

A] 1 μF

B] 100 pF

C] 0.01 μF

D] <u>50 μF</u>

1. An oscillator converts ....

c. power into d.c. power

c. power into a.c. power

mechanical power into a.c. power

none of the above

Answer : 2

2. In an LC transistor oscillator, the active device is ....

LC tank circuit

Biasing circuit

Transistor

None of the above

Answer : 3

3. In an LC circuit, when the capacitor is maximum, the inductor energy is ....

Minimum

Maximum

Half-way between maximum and minimum

None of the above

Answer : 1

4. In an LC oscillator, the frequency of oscillator is .... L or C.

Proportional to square of

Directly proportional to

Independent of the values of

Inversely proportional to square root of

Answer : 4

5. An oscillator produces................ oscillations

Damped

Undamped

Modulated

None of the above

Answer : 2

6. An oscillator employs .... feedback

Positive

Negative

Neither positive nor negative

Data insufficient

Answer : 1

7. An LC oscillator cannot be used to produce .... frequencies

High

Audio

Very low

Very high

Answer : 3

8. Hartley oscillator is commonly used in ....

Radio receivers

Radio transmitters

TV receivers

None of the above

Answer : 1

9. In a phase shift oscillator, we use .... RC sections

Two

Three

Four

None of the above

Answer : 2

10. In a phase shift oscillator, the frequency determining elements are ....

L and C

R, L and C

R and C

None of the above

Answer : 3

11. A Wien bridge oscillator uses .... feedback

Only positive

Only negative

Both positive and negative

None of the above

Answer : 3

12. The piezoelectric effect in a crystal is ....

A voltage developed because of mechanical stress

A change in resistance because of temperature

A change in frequency because of temperature

None of the above

Answer : 1

13. If the crystal frequency changes with temperature, we say that crystal

has .... temperature coefficient

Positive

Zero

Negative

None of the above

Answer : 1

14. The crystal oscillator frequency is very stable due to .... of the crystal

Rigidity

Vibrations

Low Q

High Q

Answer : 4

15. The application where one would most likely find a crystal oscillator is ....

Radio receiver

Radio transmitter

AF sweep generator

None of the above

Answer : 2

16. An oscillator differs from an amplifier because it ....

Has more gain

Requires no input signal

Requires no d.c. supply

Always has the same input

Answer : 2

17. One condition for oscillation is ....

A phase shift around the feedback loop of 180o

A gain around the feedback loop of one-third

A phase shift around the feedback loop of 0o

A gain around the feedback loop of less than 1

Answer : 3

18. A second condition for oscillations is ....

A gain of 1 around the feedback loop

No gain around the feedback loop

The attention of the feedback circuit must be one-third

The feedback circuit must be capacitive

Answer : 1

19. In a certain oscillator Av = 50. The attention of the feedback circuit must be ....

1

01

10

02

Answer : 4

20. For an oscillator to properly start, the gain around the feedback loop must

initially be

1

Greater than 1

Less than 1

Equal to attenuation of feedback circuit

Answer : 2

21. In a Wien-bridge oscillator, if the resistances in the positive feedback circuit

are decreased, the frequency..........

Remains the same

Decreases

Increases

Insufficient data

Answer : 3

22. In Colpitt's oscillator, feedback is obtained ....

By magnetic induction

By a tickler coil

From the centre of split capacitors

None of the above

Answer : 3

23. The Q of the crystal is of the order of ....

100

1000

50

More than 10,000

Answer : 4

24. Quartz crystal is most commonly used in crystal oscillators because ....

It has superior electrical properties

It is easily available

It is quite inexpensive

None of the above

Answer : 1

27. .... is a fixed frequency oscillator

Phase-shift oscillator

Hartely-oscillator

Colpitt's oscillator

Crystal oscillator

Answer : 4

28. In an LC oscillator, if the value of L is increased four times, the frequency of
oscillations is ....
Increased 2 times
Decreased 4 times
Increased 4 times
Decreased 2 times
Answer : 4

29. An important limitation of a crystal oscillator is ....
Its low output
Its high Q
Less availability of quartz crystal
Its high output
Answer : 1

30. The signal generator generally used in the laboratories is ....
oscillator
Wien-bridge
Hartely
Crystal
Phase shift
Answer : 1

1.In which of the following base systems is 123 not a valid number?
(a) Base 10
(b) Base 16
(c)Base8
(d) Base 3

2. Storage of 1 KB means the following number of bytes
(a) 1000
(b)964
(c)1024
(d) 1064

3. What is the octal equivalent of the binary number:
10111101
(a)675
(b)275
(c) 572
(d) 573.

4. Pick out the CORRECT statement:

(a) In a positional number system, each symbol represents the same value irrespective of its position

(b) The highest symbol in a position number system as a value equal to the number of symbols in the system

(c) It is not always possible to find the exact binary

(d) Each hexadecimal digit can be represented as a sequence of three binary symbols.

5.The binary code of (21.125)10 is

(a) 10101.001

(b) 10100.001

(c) 10101.010

(d) 10100.111.

6.A NAND gate is called a universal logic element because

(a) it is used by everybody

(b) any logic function can be realized by NAND gates alone

(c) all the minization techniques are applicable for optimum NAND gate realization

(d) many digital computers use NAND gates.

7. Digital computers are more widely used as compared to analog computers,

because they are

(a) less expensive

(b) always more accurate and faster

(c) useful over wider ranges of problem types

(d) easier to maintain.

8. Most of the digital computers do not have floating point hardware because

(a) floating point hardware is costly

(b) it is slower than software

(c) it is not possible to perform floating point addition by hardware

(d) of no specific reason.

9. The number 1000 would appear just immediately after

(a) FFFF (hex)

(b) 1111 (binary)

(c) 7777 (octal)

(d) All of the above.

10. (1(10101)2 is

(a) $(37)10$

(b) $(69)10$

(c) $(41)10$

(d) $- (5)10$

11. The number of Boolean functions that can be generated by n variables is equal to

(a) 2n

(b) 2^{2n}

(c) 2n-1

(d) — 2n

12. Consider the representation of six-bit numbers by two's complement, one's complement, or by sign and magnitude: In which representation is there overflow from the addition of the integers 011000 and 011000?

(a) Two's complement only

(b) Sign and magnitude and one's complement only

(c) Two's complement and one's complement only

(d) All three representations.

13. A hexadecimal odometer displays F 52 F. The next reading will be

(a)F52E

(b)G52F

(c)F53F

(d)F53O.

14. Positive logic in a logic circuit is one in which

(a) logic 0 and 1 are represented by 0 and positive voltage respectively

(b) logic 0 and, -1 are represented by negative and positive voltages respectively

(c) logic 0 voltage level is higher than logic 1 voltage level

(d) logic 0 voltage level is lower than logic 1 voltage level.

15. Which of the following gate is a two-level logic gate

(a) OR gate

(b) NAND gate

(c) EXCLUSIVE OR gate

(d) NOT gate.

16. Among the logic families, the family which can be used at very high frequency greater than 100 MHz in a 4 bit synchronous counter is

(a) TTLAS

(b) CMOS

(c)ECL

(d)TTLLS

17. An AND gate will function as OR if

(a) all the inputs to the gates are "1"

(b) all the inputs are '0'

(c) either of the inputs is "1"

(d) all the inputs and outputs are complemented.

18. An OR gate has 6 inputs. The number of input words in its truth table are

(a)6

(b)32

(c) 64

(d) 128

19. A debouncing circuit is

(a) an astable MV

(b) a bistable MV

(c) a latch

(d) a monostable MV.

20. NAND. gates are preferred over others because these

(a) have lower fabrication area

(b) can be used to make any gate

(c) consume least electronic power

(d) provide maximum density in a chip.

21. In case of OR gate, no matter what the number of inputs, a

(a) 1 at any input causes the output to be at logic 1

(b) 1 at any input causes the output to be at logic 0

(c) 0 any input causes the output to be at logic 0

(d) 0 at any input causes the output to be at logic 1.

22. The fan put of a 7400 NAND gate is

(a)2TTL

(b)5TTL

(c)8TTL

(d)10TTL

23. Excess-3 code is known as

(a) Weighted code

(b) Cyclic redundancy code

(c) Self-complementing code

(d) Algebraic code.

k24. Assuming 8 bits for data, 1 bit for parity, I start bit and 2 stop bits, the number of characters that 1200 BPS communication line can transmit is

(a) 10 CPS

(b) 120 CPS

(c) 12CPS

(d) None of the above.

1. Processor, main memory (RAM), hard disk, CD/DVD drive, CMOS, BIOS chip, etc. are housed inside ______.

(a) input unit

(b) Central Processing Unit (CPU)

(c) output unit

(d) all of them

2. ______ contains slots for fixing/ connecting processor, main memory (RAM), hard disk, CD/DVD drive, CMOS, BIOS chip, etc.

(a) Mother board

(b) bread board

(c) key board

(d) dash board

3. A stylus used to provide input through CRT monitor is called ________.

(a) scanner

(b) digital tablet

(c) light pen

(d) printer

4. VDU is expanded as ______.

(a) Visual Display Unit

(b) Virtual Display Unit (c) Visual Deception Unit

(d) Visual Display University

5. In computer monitors, CRT stands for ______.

(a) Cadmium Ray Tube

(b) Cathode Ray Tube

(c) Cathode Ray Twist

(d) Cathode Rim

6. Cathode Ray Tube (CRT) monitor has ______ level of power consumption amongst monitors.

(a) highest

(b) lowest

(c) zero

(d) least

7. LCD is expanded as ______.

(a) Linear Crystal Display

(b) Liquid Crystal Dialog

(c) <u>Liquid Crystal Display</u>

(d) Liquid Canister Display

8. LED is expanded as ________.

(a) Linear Emitting Diode

(b) <u>Light Emitting Diode</u>

(c) Liquid Emitting Diode

(d) Light Emitting Display

9. The display of LCD monitor is ______ than that of LED monitor.

(a) lighter

(b) heavier

(c) brighter

(d) <u>duller</u>

10. Height to width ratio of a monitor screen is called ______.

(a) <u>aspect ratio</u>

(b) length ratio

(c) width ratio

(d) diagonal ratio

11. Generally, CRT monitors had aspect ratio of ______.

(a) 16:9

(b) <u>4:3</u>

(c) 16:10

(d) 1:1

12. The type of printer which hits the paper to produce print is called ______.

(a) monitor

(b) scanner

(c) non-impact type printer

(d) <u>impact type printer</u>

13. The type of printer which does not hit the paper to produce print is called ______.

(a) monitor

(b) scanner

(c) <u>non-impact type printer</u>

(d) impact type printer

14. Dot matrix printer belongs to ________ category.

(a) monitor

(b) scanner

(c) non-impact type printer

(d) <u>impact type printer</u>

15. LASER printer, ink jet printer, thermal printer and plotter belong to ______ category.

(a) monitor

(b) scanner

(c) <u>non-impact type printer</u>

(d) impact type printer

16. Thermal printer uses ______ coated paper, which turns black when heat is applied.

(a) chromium

(b) <u>BisPhenol</u>

(c) nickel

(d) toner powder

17. The unit which splits power supply to various voltages required for their units of a computer is called ______ .

(a) transformer

(b) <u>Switch Mode Power Supply (SMPS)</u>

(c) transistor

(d) transducer

18. Full form for SMPS in computer is ______.

(a) Sync Mode Power Supply

(b) <u>Switch Mode Power Supply</u>

(c) Stake Mode Power Supply

(d) Switch Mode Power Socket

19. In a desktop computer, ______ produces radio frequency interference.

(a) SMPS

(b) <u>Micro-Processor</u>

(c) RAM

(d) Mouse

20. The opening provided in the front panel or rear panel of a CPU for connecting peripherals is called ______.

(a) socket

(b) pin

(c) <u>port</u>

(d) part

21. External dialup MODEM can be connected to a computer using ______ port.
(a) <u>RS232/ serial</u>
(b) PS/2
(c) VGA
(d) LPT

22. Old style (SIMPLEX) printer (like dot matrix printer) may be connected to a computer using ______ port.
(a) RS232/ serial
(b) PS/2
(c) VGA
(d) <u>LPT</u>

23. Modern (DUPLEX) printer (like LASER jet, inkjet printers) may be connected to a computer using ______ port.
(a) RS232/
(b) <u>USB</u>
(c) PS/2
(d) VGA

24. Broadband connection may be connected through ______ port.
(a) <u>RJ45/ Ethernet</u>
(b) USB
(c) PS/2
(d) VGA

25. Printer, fax machine, scanner, web camera, external DVD writer, external hard disk, etc. can be connected to computer using ______ port.
(a) RJ45
(b) <u>USB</u>
(c) PS/2
(d) VGA

26. Joystick can be connected to computer using ______ port.
(a) 3.5mm jack
(b) RJ11
(c) RJ45
(d) <u>Game</u>

27. PS/2 stands for ______.
(a) Registered Jack 11
(b) Registered Jack 45
(c) <u>Personal System 2</u>

(d) Recommended Standard 232

28. RJ11 stands for ______.

(a) <u>Registered Jack 11</u>

(b) Registered Jack 45

(c) Personal System 2

(d) Recommended Standard 232

29. RJ45 stands for ______ .

(a) Registered Jack 11

(b) <u>Registered Jack 45</u>

(c) Personal System 2

(d) Recommended Standard

30. RS232 stands for ______.

(a) Registered Jack 11

(b) Registered Jack 45

(c) Personal System 2

(d) <u>Recommended Standard 232</u>

31. RJ45 port is otherwise called ______.

(a) <u>Ethernet</u>

(b) LPT

(c) USB

(d) VGA

32. IEEE 1392 port is otherwise called ______

(a) Ethernet

(b) LPT

(c) USB

(d) <u>Firewire</u>

33. LPT stands for ______.

(a) Registered Jack 11

(b) Registered Jack 45

(c) <u>Line Printer Terminal</u>

(d) Recommended Standard 232

34. USB stands for ______.

(a) Registered Jack 11

(b) Registered Jack 45

(c) Line Printer Terminal

(d) <u>Universal Serial Bus</u>

35. High definition graphics output may be taken from port of a PC.

(a) 3.5mm jack

(b) <u>HDMI</u>

(c) RJ45

(d) LPT

36. HDMI stands for

(a) Registered Jack

(b) <u>High Definition Multimedia Interface</u>

(c) Line Printer Terminal

(d) Universal Serial Bus

37. The device primarily used to provide hardcopy is the

a) CRT

b) Computer Console

c) <u>Printer</u>

d) Card Reader

38. Dot-matrix, Deskjet, Inkjet and Laser are all types of which computer peripherals?

a) <u>Printers</u>

b) Software

c) Monitors

d) Keyboards

39. Laser printer belong to

a) line printer

b) <u>page printer</u>

c) band printer

d) dot matrix printer

40. A joystick is primarily used for

a) control sound on the screen

b) <u>Computer gaming</u>

c) enter text

d) draw pictures

41. USB refers to

a) a storage

b) a processor

c) <u>a port type</u>

d) a serial bus standard

42. The ____ may also be called the screen or monitor.

a) printer

b) scanner

c) hard disk

d) <u>display</u>

43. Speed of the printer is limited by the speed of

a) paper movement

b) <u>cartridge used</u>

c) length of paper

d) all of these

44. The OCR recognizes the ___ of the characters with the help of light source.

a) size

b) <u>shape</u>

c) colour

d) used ink

45. Laser printer belong to

a) Line printer

b) <u>page printer</u>

c) band printer

d) dot matrix printer

46. A device used for video games, flight simulators, training simulators and for controlling industrial robots.

a) Mouse

b) Light pen

c) <u>Joystick</u>

d) keyboard

47. The unattached interactive information systems such as automatic teller machine or ATM is called as ______

a) <u>Kiosks</u>

b) Sioks

c) Cianto

d) Kiaks

48. ______ help prevent power surges.

a) <u>Surge suppressor</u>

b) Spike protector

c) UPS system

d) High-grade multi-meter

49. If the memory slots have 30 pins then the chip is a?

a) DIMM

b) <u>SIMM</u>

c) SDRAM

d) All of these

50. Laser jet printer speeds are measured in pages per minute (ppm) what do we use to measure dot-matrix printers?

a) lines per inch

b) lines per sheet

c) characters per inch

d) <u>characters per second</u>

51. For a Macintosh to print successfully, the System Folder must contain:

a) File sharing software

b) A printer enabler

c) The apple Garamond font set

d) <u>A printer driver</u>

52. Which component must be vacuumed or replaced during preventative maintenance on a laserprinter?

a) Scanning mirror

b) Toner cartridge

c) <u>Ozone filter</u>

d) All of these

53. Which device uses a DMA channel?

a) Modem

b) Network Card

c) <u>Sound Card</u>

d) All of these

54.A modem could be attached to which port?

a) <u>Parallel port</u>

b) ASYNC port

c) Keyboard connector

d) Video port

55. What device prevents power interruptions, resulting in corrupted data?

a) <u>Battery back-up unit</u>

b) Surge protector

c) Multiple SIMMs strips

d) Data guard system

56. SCSI must be terminated with?

a) Dip switch

b) <u>Resister</u>

c) BNC

d) All of these

57. What?s the best way to prevent damaging your PC with static electricity?

a) place your PC on a rubber mat

b) wear leather soled shoes

c) periodically touch a safe ground point on the PC to discharge yourself

d) <u>wear an ESD wrist strap</u>

58. Which would you do first when troubleshooting a faulty monitor?

a) <u>Check its connections to the computer and power source</u>

b) Power down the monitor, then turn it on again to see if that corrects the problem

c) Use a meter to check the CRT and internal circuitry for continuity

d) None of these

59. What do you need to check serial and parallel port?

a) Port adapter

b) Logic probe

c) <u>Loopback plug</u>

d) All of these

60. You have a PC with no video* Which of the following is LEAST likely to be causing the problem?

a) defective RAM (bank zero)

b) defective microprocessor

c) <u>crashed hard drive</u>

d) loose video card

61. You get a CMOS checksum error during bootup. What is most likely the cause?

a) Power supply is bad

b) BIOS needs updating

c) <u>CMOS battery is nearing end of life</u>

d) None of these

62. Which should you use for cleaning Mylar-protected LCD screens?

a) Ammonia window cleaner

b) <u>Non-abrasive cleanser</u>

c) Anti-static wipes

d) Alcohol-impregnated wipes

63. What could cause a fixed disk error?

a) No-CD installed

b) Bad Ram

c) Slow processor

d) <u>Incorrect CMOS settings</u>

64. What is the most significant difference between the USB and IEEE 1394 standards?

a) <u>IEEE 1394 is faster</u>

b) USB does not support

c) USB is plug and play

d) IEEE 1394 is not swappable

65. When connecting two internal SCSI hard disks to a computer, where do you connect the second hard drive?

a) <u>Any open SCSI port on the computer</u>

b) A serial port on the first host adapter

c) An open parallel port on the computer

d) An open SCSI port on the first hard drive

66. When connecting a ribbon cable to a connector, how do you know which direction to plug it in?

a) The red line in the cable goes to the highest pin number

b) <u>The colored line in the cable goes to pin #1</u>

c) It does not matter

d) None of these

67. What is the first step in diagnosing a completely dead computer at the client site that was working the day before.

a) Test the power supply

b) replace the CMOS battery

c) <u>check the AC outlet</u>

d) reseat the hard drive controller cable

68. What specification covers PC hard cards?

a) SCSI

b) ISA

c) <u>PCMCIA</u>

d) MFM

69. Which common bus specification provides the fastest data transfer rate?

a) VL bus

b) ISA

c) <u>PCI</u>

d) All of these

70. Modems use transmission.
a) Synchronous
b) <u>Asynchronous</u>
c) timed interval
d) ata

71. A 6xx indicates a problem with the:
a) <u>floppy drive</u>
b) hard drive
c) keyboard
d) CD ROM

72. During preventative maintenance on a dot matrix printer, do NOT lubricate:
a) Platen assembly
b) Print head pulley
c) <u>Print head pins</u>
d) Paper advance gear bushings

73. You see the message "invalid media device" after installing a new hard drive. What do you do next?
a) <u>Format</u>
b) Fdisk
c) Partition
d) Add the OS

74. A workstation has just been installed on an Ethernet LAN, but cannot communicate with the network. What should you check first?
a) reinstall the network protocols
b) reinstall the network interface card driver
c) verify the ip configuration on the workstation
d) <u>verify the link status on the computers network card</u>

75. One of the major components of a PC is the Central Processing Unit (CPU) Which can be best described as:
a) The device that sends the monitor signals telling it what to display
b) The area that regulates all of the system power usage
c) The area where ail the of the Basic input/output routines are stored
d) <u>The area where all of the processing takes place</u>

76. Which monitor would provide the highest level of performance?
a) VGA
b) XGA
c) CGA

d) <u>SVGA</u>

77. Which of the following items would require you to comply with EPA disposal guidelines?

a) Keyboard

b) System board

c) Power supply

d) <u>Battery</u>

78. A hard disk is divided into tracks which are further subdivided into:

a) clusters

b) <u>sectors</u>

c) vectors

d) heads

79. What is the paper feeding technology most commonly associated with dot-matrix printers?

a) sheet feed

b) <u>tractor feed</u>

c) friction feed

d) manual feed

80. Which step should you perform first before discharging a CRT?

a) Remove the CRT from its housing

b) Disconnect the CRT from the computer

c) Remove the video assembly

d) <u>Turn power off before removing power source</u>

81. A capacitor is measured in which of the following units?

a) Volts

b) Ohms

c) <u>Farads</u>

d) Resistance

82. What would you ask to determine if the display is working?

a) Is there a video cursor or action on the screen?

b) Did the computer beep or chime?

c) Is there high voltage static on the screen

d) <u>All of these</u>

83. Your CD-ROM audio cable connects to the:

a) speaker

b) <u>sound card (or motherboard if sound is integrated with it)</u>

c) power supply

d) hard drive

84. Type one PC cards:

a) are used only in desktops

b) are no longer being produced

c) <u>are the thinnest of the PC cards</u>

d) don?t exist

85. In laser technology, what happens during the transfer stage? a) Residual toner is transferred to the waste receptacle

b) The laser transfers the image from the drum to the paper

c) <u>The image is transferred from the drum to the paper</u>

d) A negative charge is transferred to the surface to the drum

86. Suppose that the power lamp is on, but the printer will not print. What can you do to correct the problem?

a) <u>Make sure the printer is on line</u>

b) Replace the AC line fuse

c) Turn the printer on and off

d) Replace the ribbon

87. A dialog box with a bomb appears on a Macintosh screen. What type of problem has occurred?

a) A RAM problem

b) A software problem

c) A ROM problem

d) An ADB problem

88. What can you use to ensure power is not interrupted, resulting in corrupted data?

a) <u>UPS</u>

b) Propergrounding

c) Surge protector

d) Sag protector

89. A 25-pin female connector on the back of your computer will typically be:

a) Serial port 1

b) <u>A parallel port</u>

c) Docking

d) COM2 port

90. What is the recommended way to fix the registry description for the printer driver

a) Delete the spool file

b) Run regedit.exe and remove any reference to the printers

c) Run sysedit.exe and remove any reference to the printers

d) <u>Remove the printer driver and re-install it</u>

91. An important first step in troubleshooting which component in a laser printer is causing a jam is to:

a) <u>note where in the paper path the paper stops</u>

b) check all voltages

c) look up error codes

d) turn the printer off, then on again

92. What is the size of the reserved memory area?

a) 64 kb

b) <u>384 kb</u>

c) 640 kb

d) 1024 kb

93. Dust in a computer actually increase the size of the magnetic fields inside it. This is not good, so you must occasionaly dust, I trust. What?s the best way to do this?

a) reservevaccum

b) any small vaccum device

c) blow real hard on the system board

d) <u>use compressed air can</u>

94. A parity error usually indicates a problem with:

a) <u>memory</u>

b) hard drive

c) hard drive controller

d) I/O controller

95. The monitor power LED is „on? but the monitor screen is completely dark. The least likely cause of the problem is:

a) Defect in the computers video circuitry

b) Disconnected video cable

c) Defective monitor

d) <u>System RAM problem</u>

96. How is ink transferred to paper in common ink jet printers?

a) Boiling ink

b) <u>Crystal</u>

c) Motorized pump

d) Ink is sprayed on the paper and managed by a nozzle

97. In Inkjet printers, what is the most common problem with the paper tray?

a) inconsistent printing

b) <u>malfunctioning pick-up rollers</u>

c) misalignment of the sheet feeder

d) paper jamming on the ink cartridge

98. A customer calls and says her computer won?t boot, she can hear noises and can see lights on the box, but nothing comes up on the screen, what should you take to the site to fix the problem?

a) hard drive

b) <u>video card</u>

c) power cable

d) power supply

99. What action will correct patchy, faint, uneven or intermittent print on a dot matrix printer?

a) <u>Replacing the ribbon</u>

b) Replacing the timing belt

c) Adjusting the paper feed tension

d) Adjusting the tractor feed ransion

100. Every video card must have?

a) CMOS

b) <u>RAM</u>

c) CPU

d) All of these

101. Which best describes a fragmented hard drive:

a) The platters are bad

b) Data files are corrupted

c) Clusters of data are damaged

d) <u>Files are not stored in consecutive clusters</u>

102. A laser printer generates a totally black page, what is the cause?

a) malfunctioning imaging laser

b) low level in the toner cartridge

c) no power to transfer corona

d) <u>no power to the primary corona</u>

103. You must service the laser printer in your office. Which part of the printer should you avoid touching because it is hot?

a) <u>Fuser</u>

b) Printer head

c) primary corona

d) High voltage power supply

104. During the normal PC boot process, which of the following is active first?

a) RAM BIOS

b) CMOS

c) ROM BIOS

d) Hard disk information

105. Which device should not be plugged into a standard ups?

a) monitor

b) laser printer

c) ink-jet printer

d) an external modem

106. What allows you to print on both sides of the printer?

a) fuser

b) duplexer

c) toner cartridge

d) paper-swapping unit

107. Which is NOT typically a field Replaceable Unit?

a) System ROM

b) Power supply

c) System chasis

d) Video controller

108. Which is the easiest component to environmentally recycle?

a) Motherboards

b) CMOS batteries

c) Toner cartridges

d) Cathode ray tubes

109. What problem can occur if a printer cable is to close to a power cable?

a) ESD Electrostatic Discharge

b) EMI Electromagnetic Interference

c) parity error

d) no affect

110. How can you totally protect a PC from damage during an electrical storm?

a) Disconnect the AC power cable

b) Disconnect all external cables and power cords

c) Use a surge protector

d) Turn off the AC power

111. All operating systems get their total memory initialized from? a) CPU

b) <u>BIOS</u>

c) ROM

d) RAM

112. During the fusing process, toner is:

a) dry pressed into the paper

b) electrically bonded to the paper

c) melted into the paper

d) <u>high pressure sprayed onto the paper</u>

113. After you service a laser printer, you notice dirty print. Which of the following would correct the problem?

a) Clean the developer tank

b) Reset the printer

c) <u>Run several blank pages</u>

d) Clean the laser diode

114. During the boot process, a system first counts memory from where?

a) Expansion memory board

b) Video adapter

c) <u>System board</u>

d) Cache

115. You have a system that periodically locks up. You have ruled out software, and now suspect that it is hardware. What should you do first that could help you narrow it down to the component at fault?

a) rotate the RAM

b) replace the RAM

c) replace the level 2 cache SIMM

d) <u>disable the CPU cache in CMOS</u>

116. What is the best way to protect your hard drive data?

a) <u>regular backups</u>

b) periodically defrag it

c) runchkdsk at least once a week

d) run a regular diagnostic

117. Missing slot covers on a computer can cause?

a) <u>over heat</u>

b) power surges

c) EMI

d) incomplete path for ESD

118. In laser printer technology, what happens during the conditioning stage?

a) The corona wire places a uniform positive charge on the paper

b) <u>A uniform negative charge is placed on the photosensitive drum</u>

c) A uniform negative charge is placed on the toner

d) All of these

119. What product is used to clean keys on a keyboard?

a) TMC solvent

b) Silicon spray

c) Denatured alcohol

d) <u>All-purpose cleaner</u>

120. Which peripheral port provide the FASTEST throughout to laser printers?

a) RS-232

b) SCSI

c) <u>Parallel</u>

d) Serial

121. Your customer tells you the print quality of their dot matrix printer is light then dark. Which of the following could cause the problem.

a) Paper slippage

b) <u>Improper ribbon advancement</u>

c) Paper thickness

d) Head position

122. The 34-pin connection on an I/O card I for?

a) <u>Floppy drive</u>

b) SCSI drive

c) IDE drive

d) Zip drive

123. The terms "red book", "yellow book" and "orange book" refer to:

a) SCSI

b) IDE

c) Floppy drive technology

d) <u>CD-ROM standards</u>

124. What beep codes could indicate a system board or power supply failure?

a) steady short beep

b) no beep

c) one long continuous beep tone

d) <u>All of these</u>

125. Which part of the laser printer should NOT be exposed to sunlight?

a) Transfer corona assembly

b) <u>PC drum</u>

c) Primary corona wire

d) Toner cartridge

126. In inkjet technology the droplets on ink are deflected by?

a) <u>multi directional nozzles</u>

b) electronically charges plates

c) high pressure plates

d) electro static absorbtion

127. Which provide the fastest access to large video files?

a) Optical drives

b) IDE hard drives

c) <u>SCSI hard drives</u>

d) EIDE hard drives

128. A 25-pin female connector on the back of your computer will typically be:

a) Serial port 1

b) <u>A parallel port</u>

c) Docking

d) COM2 port

129. On the PC side, the printer port is a:

a) 25 pin female serial connector

b) 15 pin female parallel connector

c) 25 pin male serial connector

d) <u>25 pin female parallel connector</u>

130. You are installing an application in Windows 95, and the computer crashes, what do you do?

a) Press alt + Ctrl + delete, twice

b) press alt + Ctrl + delete, and end task

c) press the reset button on the computer

d) <u>turn off computer and boot from a floppy disk</u>

131. RS-232 is a standard that applies to:

a) <u>serial ports</u>

b) parallel ports

c) game ports

d) networks

132. You just installed a new IDE hard drive, but your system BIOS will not recognize the new drive, what should you check first.

a) cable sequence

b) <u>jumpers on the hard drive</u>

c) drivers that need to be loaded

d) hard drive manufacturer web site information

133. All the physical components of a computer are collectively called .

(a) software

(b) <u>hardware</u>

(c) malware

(d) junkware

134. Hardware _____ be touched.

(a) cannot

(b) <u>can</u>

(c) may

(d) would

135. Hardware _____ electric power for working.

(a) <u>consumes</u>

(b) does not consume

(c) generates (d) creates

136. Hardware _____ space.

(a) does not occupy

(b) <u>occupies</u>

(c) does not require

(d) does not need

www.ingramcontent.com/pod-product-compliance
Ingram Content Group UK Ltd.
Pitfield, Milton Keynes, MK11 3LW, UK
UKHW021907190726
13853UKWH00002B/559